THE
TWENTY-FIVE
DAYS

THE
TWENTY-FIVE
DAYS

JOHN MASEFIELD

with a new introduction

by

Jon Cooksey

Pen & Sword
MILITARY

First published in Great Britain in 1941
Published in this format in 2004 by
Pen & Sword Military
an imprint of
Pen & Sword Books Ltd
47 Church Street
Barnsley
South Yorkshire
S70 2AS

ISBN 1 84415 037 2

A CIP catalogue record for this book is
available from the British Library

Typeset in 11/13 Sabon by
Phoenix Typesetting, Auldgirth, Dumfriesshire

Printed and bound in England by CPI UK

Pen & Sword Books Ltd incorporates the Imprints of Pen & Sword
Aviation, Pen & Sword Maritime, Pen & Sword Military, Wharncliffe
Local History, Pen & Sword Select, Pen & Sword Military Classics and
Leo Cooper.

For a complete list of Pen & Sword titles please contact
PEN & SWORD BOOKS LIMITED
47 Church Street, Barnsley, South Yorkshire, S70 2AS, England
E-mail: enquiries@pen-and-sword.co.uk
Website: www.pen-and-sword.co.uk

Contents

Introduction
by
Jon Cooksey

The 1st June 1940 was John Masefield's birthday. Under more normal circumstances it should have been a day of celebration for the Masefield family. Not only had the established and popular writer turned sixty-two but also his birthday had come just days after passing a significant ten-year milestone in his career as the nation's Poet Laureate. But it was not a time for celebration on the national stage. Britain had been at war for almost nine months and although, from a cursory glance at the headlines of the last few days, Masefield could have been forgiven for thinking that the British Army had secured a notable victory in its recent campaign against the Germans in northern France and Flanders, the reality, as is so often the case, was much more disturbing. Even as the red-masted dailies trumpeted the return of Britain's 'glorious' and 'unbeatable' heroes to a shocked public hitherto starved of information regarding the performance of its Field Force on the continent, the grim truth was that militarily the British, along with their French allies, had been comprehensively routed.

The entire Flanders campaign, from the moment the German onslaught had begun at dawn on 10th May until the official termination of Operation Dynamo – the evacuation of the British Field Force and thousands of French troops – on the afternoon of 4th June, had been spectacularly short. It had taken a little over twenty-five days. Even so, at this most bleak of moments in British history, something – nebulous at first – began to crystallize in the British mindset. As Poet Laureate, John Masefield determined to capture something of what was happening and thus record it for the nation.

1

He could write verse certainly – that's what Poets Laureate had done since the time of Dryden, the first incumbent – but, as a writer first and foremost, he could do more. He could develop a narrative work on the Flanders campaign.

By late July his mind was made up. He would write a book, based on official sources for which official permission would be sought. The events that unfolded during the months following Masefield's decision, tell a unique story – a story which, after more than sixty years, is now revealed for the first time – of a remarkable breakdown of communications, misunderstandings and security fears within the higher echelons of the Civil Service. It is a story of intrigue and propaganda, of censorship, suppression and the eventual destruction of the work of an intensely patriotic Poet Laureate, driven to record the service and sacrifice of his British heroes, on the orders of those at the very highest levels of British wartime government.

It had been a little over a decade earlier, on 10th May 1930, that the press had descended on the then Masefield family home at Boars Hill near Oxford and, in a barrage of flashbulbs and questions, had probed the newly anointed Poet Laureate for his views on the importance of the Laureateship, his method of writing poetry and its purposes. Congratulatory letters had poured in then from family and friends and from some of Masefield's contemporaries, stars of the literary firmament in their own right who had also been eligible for the prestigious position.

Ramsay MacDonald, a man who himself had ploughed a new furrow as Britain's first Labour Prime Minister in 1924, broke new ground again with his nomination of Masefield as the sixteenth Poet Laureate, yet his choice was not entirely surprising. By the spring of 1930 Masefield was a well-established writer, enormously popular on both sides of the Atlantic. In a world prior to the distractions of global communications, of television, the Internet and news-stands groaning under the weight of 'celebrity' magazines, Masefield's *Collected Poems* had sold more than 100,000 copies in the seven years between 1923 and 1930 while sales of his novels *Sard Harker* (1924) and *Odtaa* (1926) also reached six figures. [1] For MacDonald, the ex-Morayshire clerk who had risen to represent the working class in parliament at the head of a Labour government, Masefield's lack of a university education, his youthful brush with poverty in

America and his well publicized views on compassion, speaking up for the dispossessed and the underdog, were most definitely in his favour.

And Masefield took his duties seriously. In his first speech as Laureate, to mark his being granted the Freedom of the City of Hereford on 23rd October 1930, he spoke of 'subtle ties, deeper than I can explain' which bound him to his native county and country. His references to the 'bounty and beauty' of 'these red ploughlands', of 'woodland and pasture and lovely brooks', of the 'bounty of Earth being the shadow of Heaven' underpinned his yearning for a return to a more simple, rustic way of life. These sentiments echoed soldier poet Edward Thomas's lifelong passion for the very earth of England and the creatures and people of the countryside, as well as the imagery in Rupert Brooke's famous poem *The Soldier*, written in 1914 at a moment of extreme danger for the country these men loved and in whose service they died – Brooke of illness on his way to Gallipoli in 1915 and Thomas from shellfire on the opening day of the British offensive at Arras in 1917.

Now, on his sixty-second birthday, more than a quarter of a century after that great European crisis that pitched Britain into a titanic struggle for survival against an aggressive and expansionist Germany, and a decade after his inauguration as Poet Laureate, John Masefield's native land and all that he held dear, teetered once again on the edge of an abyss in northern France and Flanders. The fault line ran through the French channel port of Dunkirk.

It had all happened so quickly. In September 1938, Neville Chamberlain, the then British Prime Minister, had returned from a meeting with the German Chancellor, Adolf Hitler in Munich, waving an agreement which he believed had secured 'peace for our time'. In the House of Commons Winston Churchill, who had long opposed Chamberlain's policy of appeasement, greeted the news with dismay. In tones which would later be used to galvanize the spirit of a nation and which would reverberate down the ages, he delivered his uncompromising verdict. 'England', he said, 'has been offered a choice between war and shame. She has chosen shame – and will get war'. And war is exactly what she got – but not straight away.

Less than a year after his declaration of peace, Chamberlain's hopes lay in ruins. It was Chamberlain's voice which the British people heard on their wirelesses on the bright Sunday morning of 3rd September, relaying the devastating news that, 'this country is at war with Germany', two days after the German invasion of Poland. Poland was crushed in a little over two weeks by a form of warfare the world had never seen. This was blitzkrieg – 'lightning war'. Britain and her ally France busied themselves in preparation for what they believed would be the inevitable German strike in Western Europe. The first four divisions of the British Field Force, consisting of more than 150,000 men under their Commander-in-Chief General Lord Gort V.C., was dispatched to the area of the Franco-Belgian border during the latter half of September 1939, to take up a position to the left of a French army defending the Maginot Line of fortifications on the Franco-German border. Once in position the Allies paused and held their collective breath. But nothing happened.

In Western Europe at least this was war without any 'war', a 'Phoney War'. Blitzkrieg, it seemed had been supplanted by 'sitzkrieg' – lightning war to armchair war. All that changed in the spring of 1940 when the hot breath of war blew once more, this time on Norway, and then came the hammer blow. At dawn on 10th May 1940, the Germans finally unleashed the full might of their armies to fall on France, Belgium and the Low Countries in what became one of military history's most dazzlingly brilliant operations. Blitzkrieg was visited on Europe once more.

In less than twenty days the Germans had secured the Netherlands and forced a Belgian surrender. The French and British Armies, taken completely by surprise, were separated by the advance of the German armoured divisions in the van of the assault and reeled back in the face of an adversary that had completely outmanoeuvred them. It took just ten days for the first of the German panzers to reach the sea. They had crossed the old First World War killing grounds on the Somme in a matter of hours and by 7.00 p.m. on 20th May had seized Abbeville. The German armoured *Sichelschnitt* – the scythe stroke – had cut a great swathe through the Allied forces and had created an extended 'panzer corridor' that had cut vital road and rail communications between the Allied forces to the north and south.

Time was ebbing away for the Allies. Lord Gort, convinced that the only option left open to him was to make for the channel coast, rejected the idea of breaking out southward towards the River Somme and instead organized a fighting retreat, creating a series of 'blocking' points along his army's route in an effort to secure a vital escape corridor. Gort's army headed north. It was there that his Field Force would stand and fight it out with its back to the sea.

An allied counter stroke at Arras on 21st May checked the advance of the German *panzers* and tested the resolve of Hitler and some of his generals. Bitter fighting followed. Between 22nd and 26th May, struggles for the ports of Boulogne and Calais became characterized by countless acts of selfless valour and irredeemable loss but eventually they succumbed, leaving the panzers free to roll ever onward. There appeared little now to thwart them in their primary objective, that of securing an operational and strategic feat of arms such as the world had never before witnessed by administering the *coup de grâce* to the Allied armies stumbling their weary way back to the only port now open to them – Dunkirk.

Dunkirk. There can be few more evocative place names to have been plucked from their natural homes on the Continent, transplanted in Britain and had their original meanings transformed into abstract ideas, powerful emotions, and an expression of a nation's mood by that master of appropriation, the English language. Agincourt is, perhaps another example and one could probably add Waterloo, Ypres and Somme to the list. But Dunkirk is different. Agincourt in 1415 and Waterloo 400 years later were English or British victories. At Ypres the British defenders of the 'Immortal Salient' defied the Kaiser's Armies for a little over four years from 1914–1918 and although there were appalling British losses during the Battle of the Somme in 1916, it could never in any sense be described as a defeat.

On the other hand, towards the end of May 1940, the British Army's experience at Dunkirk, in spite of Hitler's order to halt his panzers on 24th May, exhibited all the attributes of defeat. Heavy weapons and vital equipment – hundreds of vehicles, radios, thousands of tons of stores and rations and in many cases uniforms and personal weapons – all were abandoned as the Allied armies fell back towards the town with the Germans snapping at their heels. Only one thing remained; the men themselves.

Over a period of nine operational days between 6.57 p.m. on Sunday 26th May and 2.23 p.m. on Tuesday 4th June 1940 almost an entire army, along with tens of thousands belonging to another, was delivered from total annihilation by the skin of its teeth in one of the most audacious, heavily improvised and acutely hazardous sea-borne evacuations ever attempted in the history of warfare. Figures vary according to the sources consulted but the Admiralty reckoned that 338,226 Allied troops had been rescued from Dunkirk's gently shelving beaches and its harbour's eastern mole by the end of an operation that secured immortality through its code name – Dynamo. More than 215,000 of that final total were British. And this is where numbers really do count, because every man who had been snatched from the jaws of defeat at Dunkirk, ferried across the channel in a variety of craft to England and then greeted with strong, sweet tea, sandwiches, and cheers more usually reserved for victors, had lived on to fight another day. With every vessel that disgorged its load of exhausted, thirsty and ravenous troops onto the quays of the south coast channel ports, and with every line that was etched into the endless columns of grimy faces, another line of what was to become the epic of Dunkirk was written. From the moment the press were given the green light to report the evacuation on 31st May, the propaganda machine was cranked relentlessly and, line by line, the epic of Dunkirk began to pass into the realms of myth and legend as the 'unbeatable', the 'great' and the 'glorious' of the British Army returned. It also marked the point at which the 'Dunkirk spirit', and all it came to stand for, began to take root in the nation's collective psyche.

On the day the evacuation ended Winston Churchill, now Prime Minister, delivered his famous 'we shall fight on the beaches' speech to the House. Perhaps the most famous and oft quoted paragraph of that speech ended with the words 'we shall never surrender'. Whether by accident or design, every word of that short but emotive section could trace its roots back across thousands of years to the language of Old English. Every word that is, except one; 'surrender'.[2]

Churchill was at pains to warn the public that 'wars are not won by evacuations,' but he also pointed to 'a victory inside this deliverance'. Here was a defeat which could, in the best of British 'last ditch' traditions, be spun to an anxious nation as a victory for British stoicism and resolve in the face of a rampant German war machine. From that moment on, the 'Dunkirk spirit' dug deep, took hold and gripped the nation. And so, as Melvyn Bragg has so succinctly pointed out, 'into the unconscious went a place marking a defeat but by some necessity of survival, its name was subversively inspirational'.[3] It is still with us today and is invoked, like a unifying talisman, at times of national crisis.

The brevity of the campaign – marked in days, not months or years – and the tremendous national significance of what had lately taken place was not lost on the nation's Poet Laureate. Although, since the era of Queen Victoria, the serving Poet Laureate had been under no legal obligation to produce poetry to mark significant royal events or moments of national import, Masefield, who viewed himself primarily as a 'writer' rather than a 'poet', usually felt a moral duty to compose verses on such occasions. Peter Vansittart has noted that his views of war, society and history were in any case more realistic than those of some of his contemporaries. It was as though '. . . his experiences of hardship and gradual acceptance, and his feelings for a thousand years of British events, enabled him to identify with popular feelings in national crises, rejoicing and bereavements.'[4] And what other occasion, in spite of the losses incurred, could possibly be of more national import than the deliverance of more than 200,000 British soldiers – and ultimately perhaps, by extrapolation, an entire nation – from almost certain destruction at the hands of Nazi Germany?

The battlefields on which the men of this British Army had fought, and their enduring importance for the British, began to resonate in Masefield's consciousness. Here were fields over which men of Britain had fought before – Waterloo, Fontenoy, 'Wipers'. He noted these names which would eventually find a voice in verses composed after the completion of his work on *The Twenty-Five Days*.

> They marched over the Fields of Waterloo
> By Gomont and La Haie, and then fell back,
> Forever facing front to the attack
> Across the English bones.

> Westward by Fontenoy, their ranks withdrew;
> The German many bomb-bursts beat the drum;
> And many a trooper marched to kingdom come
> Upon the Flanders stones

Westward they went, past Wipers and the old
Fields bought and paid for by their brothers' blood.
Their feet were in the snapping of the flood
That sped to gulf them down.[5]

As an established writer Masefield's oeuvre consisted not only of several collections of poetry but also of novels, plays and narrative works. Towards the end of his long life, he confessed his fancy for making 'the fantastic real' in a letter to Dr Corliss Lamont. 'I am a storyteller' he wrote in 1966, 'and am always drawn to narrative.'[6] And the story of the Flanders Campaign, replete with tales of oppression, of terrified, dispossessed refugees crushed under the heels of German jackboots and the wheels of their tanks, and the gritty stories of soldiers, sailors – some in their 'little ships' – and airmen refusing to break, was a concoction that proved irresistible to a man who had experienced hardship and anxiety at first hand.

By the age of seventeen Masefield had served two years aboard the *Conway*, a school ship for boys hoping to become officers in the Merchant Navy, and had survived a thirty day battering in mountainous seas whilst 'rounding the Horn' as an apprentice aboard the *Gilcraux*, a four-masted barque of the White Star Line. He had written about the sea and returning heroes before, now he would do it again.

At some point during the latter part of June and July 1940 it appears that he was indeed 'drawn to narrative', and the idea of a book became fixed in his mind. By the end of July he had announced to C.S. Evans, the Managing Director of his publisher, William Heinemann, that he was writing it.[7]

After all, Masefield was no stranger to war or indeed writing about war. Like Edward Thomas or Rupert Brooke, whose love of England he shared, he had volunteered for active service at the start of the First World War but had been rejected on health grounds. That did not prevent him from crossing to France in the wake of many thousands of his countrymen. By February of 1915 he was serving as a medical orderly in a British Red Cross hospital at the Chateau d'Arc en Barrois, south of Chaumont, sixty miles behind the French front in the Haute Marne. There he had worked long hours under trying conditions during the early spring of 1915, carrying out menial tasks and caring for wounded French soldiers;

sometimes assisting with amputations and performing the grisly, but necessary, task of burning the severed limbs. The grinding pace and emotional expenditure had taken their toll and the work had almost exhausted him by the time he returned to England towards early summer, but Masefield refused to rest. He immediately busied himself in trying to raise the £3,500 necessary to equip a travelling field hospital which he planned to take over to the Argonne sector, again behind the French front. That enterprise came to nought but he had received sufficient offers of support to respond with enthusiasm when his erstwhile employers, the British Red Cross Society, approached him again to lead an expedition on its behalf in the summer of 1915. They had received an urgent call for reinforcements for the motor boat ambulance service which plied the sixty-mile stretch of the Aegean Sea back and forth between Mudros Bay, on the island of Lemnos, and the Dardanelles Peninsular, evacuating wounded British and French soldiers from the trenches of another theatre of war. He was bound for Gallipoli.

With his boyhood maritime experience standing him in good stead, Masefield set out at the head of a flotilla of four small craft on a voyage, via Gibraltar and Malta, which took several weeks. What he saw and experienced of the conditions both at Mudros, and at Anzac beach on the peninsular itself, during his brief visit dismayed him. Like almost everyone else serving on that baking, parched and fly blown peninsular during the summer of 1915, he was plagued by lice, fleas and shrapnel and suffered from a severe bout of dysentery which reduced his weight by sixteen pounds. Coming as it did, on top of the exhaustion wrought by his earlier service behind the Western Front, he was a shadow of himself by the time he returned home in mid-October and confessed to feeling 'very old'. By the end of December, however, he had recovered sufficiently to embark on an extensive lecture tour of the United States, pre-publicity for which had billed him as 'The Sailor Poet'. His experiences of Gallipoli had by now seeped into his storyteller's soul and he took them with him when he crossed the Atlantic early in 1916. He arrived in New York on 12th January just three days after the last of the British troops had been spirited away from Gallipoli.

It could be said that Masefield had already 'done his bit' practically; now here was an opportunity to serve his country on the intellectual front. The United States was still neutral and certain regions, particularly the mid-west, were seen as hotbeds of pro-German sentiment. Urged on by Canadian born Sir Gilbert Parker, one of the senior figures in the highly secretive propaganda and intelligence department based at Wellington House, Masefield realized that he could use his tour to gauge American public opinion in relation to the war, whilst at the same time countering German propaganda by putting the case for the Allied cause from a uniquely British perspective. This he did, but he was surprised at the number of hecklers who frequently tackled him about the 'debacle' that had been the Gallipoli expedition. Submitting a formal report to the Foreign Office on his return to Britain in March 1916, he proposed that he write an article on Gallipoli to dispel the lies engendered by, as he put it, 'the Boche taint' of German propaganda. The article grew into a book – Masefield was allowed access to brigade and battalion war diaries – titled simply *Gallipoli*, which was published in August 1916 as a means of explaining the campaign for bereaved families at home as well as an American audience. The tragic/heroic story of the hazardous amphibious invasion and the equally hazardous, but brilliantly planned and executed amphibious evacuation of large numbers of Allied troops drew on the saltwater flowing in Masefield's veins. Wreathed in romance and legend, *Gallipoli*'s pages were, are, filled with romantic heroes struggling to overcome every burden that the Turks, the elements and even their own governments could heap upon them, yet still they emerge, bowed but unbeaten and with their spirit unbroken. It sold like hotcakes both in England and the States and went some way to pouring oil on the troubled transatlantic waters of discontent concerning the details of the nine-month offensive. At home it was hailed as a triumph. It was, however, by necessity, only a partial story. Masefield was too close in time to the events about which he had written and the strict censorship still in force ensured that large and important pieces of the jigsaw were left out. But if the Gallipoli experience had proved anything at all it had proved that very large numbers of men, – 118,316 in all – thousands of animals and several hundred guns and vehicles, could be lifted from an alien shore in a difficult amphibious evacuation with minimal casualties. It remains a remarkable military feat by the standards of any age and a template was forged when the last lighter sailed away from W Beach at 4 a.m. on the morning of 9th January 1916 before the British detonated their abandoned magazines to terminate the expedition in spectacular fashion. The British would return to study that template a quarter of a century later. Masefield, too, had set a template with his story of the campaign and would be struck by the many parallels when the time came to replace the name 'Gallipoli' with that of 'Dunkirk'.

The runaway success of *Gallipoli* was by no means the end of Masefield's career as a 'war writer', quite the contrary. In August 1916 he crossed to France once more, again under the aegis of Sir Gilbert Parker's department, to research American voluntary aid to the Allies and it was towards the end of his 'tour' of duty in October that he met Lord Esher. *Gallipoli*'s popular appeal had, like a shooting star, streaked across the channel and into the orbit of the de facto head of the shadowy British intelligence community in Paris and further, had attracted the attention of none other than the usually taciturn Commander-in-Chief of the British Army, Sir Douglas Haig.

Haig, said Esher, had expressly requested the services of Masefield for a pressing and momentous task, a task for which he would be provided with every 'facility'. He was needed on the Somme battlefield, he wrote to his wife Constance, 'to write the Chronicle of the big attack from the very beginning'.[8] In Masefield's view the epic struggle still raging on the chalk downlands of Picardy had even replaced Gallipoli as a 'grand event' and had become 'the biggest thing' that 'England' had been engaged in. Thus, Masefield reasoned, it had to become 'a possession of the English mind forever'.[9]

Masefield arrived on the Somme to begin his preparatory work surveying the terrain on 17th October on the last day of the Battle of the Ancre Heights, although the Battle of the Somme in its entirety still had more than a month left to run. He met Haig and began to walk many of the blasted wastelands that had once been sleepy rural backwaters – Beaumont Hamel, Thiepval, Pozières, Delville Wood – 'hallowed acres' which became sacred ground for Britain and its Empire.

He returned to the Somme early in 1917, in khaki this time with the honorary, and therefore unpaid, rank of Second Lieutenant, and worked non-stop, visiting and re-visiting the battlefield, hoping to talk to the men as time and circumstance allowed. He remained until mid-May and returned to England eager to start work. He planned and completed a preface – a study of the topography of the battle-field based on his walking tours of the British front line at the start of the offensive – but ultimately his grand design for a 'Chronicle' based on Sir Douglas Haig's commission was doomed. Promised the use of official papers, when it came to the crunch Whitehall closed its ranks and its doors. And the doors remained firmly barred.

There was little Masefield could do but persuade Heinemann to publish his preface as a book in its own right. *The Old Front Line* – brief at only 128 pages long – appeared in December 1917 to be followed, in 1919, by *The Battle of the Somme*, an even slimmer volume. At ninety-eight pages it could hardly claim to be the broad canvas on which Masefield had envisaged layering his exhaustive work. Denied access to detailed war diaries, official documents and extensive interviews with the men involved, he wrote what he could from memory and his own notes. Inevitably, the resulting book could never be more than a seasoned author's sketch of a momentous event viewed through a peephole. His disappointment at not being allowed access to the sources he had been promised was intense but it was not to be Masefield's final encounter with the labyrinthine machinations of Whitehall and the 'cold shoulder' offered by some of the mandarins who stalked the corridors of power.

Whether any lingering memories of that official obstruction came back to haunt Masefield as he sat down, more than twenty years later, to type a letter to Sir Stephen Gaselee, the Foreign Office Librarian, requesting information for a new book, we shall never know. Masefield wanted clarification on several points.

Dear Sir Stephen Gaselee,

It is just possible, that you may remember shewing me the Pepys Library many years ago, when I was staying with Goldie Dickinson.

I am now writing to ask your help in obtaining access to some Foreign Office Archives.

Professor Woodward, of All Souls, has said, that perhaps you would be able to give this help.

I have been asked to write the story of the recent campaign which ended at Dunquerque. *(sic)* I am anxious to give precise details on the following points :-

A. The exact promise given to the French by this country, as to military help in the event of war. How many divisions did we covenant to send, how many guns, squadrons, etc?

Enemy propaganda is very busy on this point already.

B. The nature of the refusals of Holland and Belgium to consider Staff Talks with our General Staffs before and during the war.

C. The lengths to which those two lands pushed their rigourous neutrality, and the nature of the insults offered to them by Germany, ships sunk, seamen murdered, and frontiers violated, etc.

D. The nature of the appeals made to us by King Leopold, or his Government, for help on the 10th May.

E. The precise excuse offered by the Germans, (if any), for their violation of Holland and Belgium.

F. Any words of regret or extenuation offered by King Leopold for his surrender.

Perhaps if these papers may be seen in the volumes of Confidential Prints, you could allow me to see them?

I have to be in London on Monday afternoon next; and could come up on any other day next week.

Any help of the kind would be most useful.

Yours sincerely,

John Masefield.[10]

It was 24th July 1940 and these were uncertain times for Britain. The majority of the British Army, routed in France, was, at least, safely back from Dunkirk. France, thoroughly beaten, had fallen. The Germans had entered Paris on 14th June and Hitler had even toured the French capital. The French had a new Prime Minister; eighty-four year-old Marshal Henri Philippe Pétain, hero of Verdun, rallying point for the doves of the French government who had sued for peace with Germany and bitter critic of the British decision to evacuate its army from France in order to fight on. On 20th June, in one of his early radio broadcasts as Premier, Pétain's anger at his perceived lack of British support finally boiled over. Seeking to explain the French defeat he lamented 'In May 1918 we had eighty-five British divisions; in May 1940 there were only ten.'[11]

Nor had the danger yet passed for Britain. With France and the Low Countries subdued there was every expectation that the Battle for Britain was imminent. German propaganda was eagerly fanning the continental flames of suspicion and anger directed at a self-serving and 'perfidious Albion', and transmitting the results to anyone who would listen.

The Poet Laureate's request, received by Sir Stephen the following day and entered into the Foreign Office's registry under reference, 'C (Germany) 7960/7960/18', stirred up a hornet's nest and triggered a flurry of official minutes which created a paper trail that fluttered its way through several government departments, ministries and the War Cabinet Office and ultimately led to the Prime Minister himself. It is little wonder then, that as Sir Stephen scanned Masefield's letter closely, it immediately set alarm bells ringing. Gaselee underlined the words 'asked to' in Masefield's fourth paragraph and, in the left hand margin, scribbled 'by who?'

Masefield did not travel to London to meet Gaselee the following week or the week after. On 13th August, almost three weeks later, Masefield again wrote to Sir Stephen enquiring whether it would be '. . . now possible to look at the confidential papers about which I wrote to you towards the end of July?' Still there was no response. The Foreign Office file had begun its rounds.

The initial minute by Mr. Warr appears to view Masefield's queries as minor but rather troublesome itches that required scratching and disposing of. It was suggested that the Political Intelligence Department of the Foreign Office be approached to produce a composite response. But before any commitment to assist Masefield could be made, opinions regarding his request had to be collated.

It becomes evident, on reading the minutes, that as the paper began to circulate in the Foreign Office its members became increasingly concerned and uneasy about the methods of gathering and then releasing possibly sensitive information to Masefield, without first considering how best it may be presented, lest it damage Britain's long-term interests and international relation-ships. Nations had recently been brought to their knees and humiliated in very public shows of German supremacy. National wounds were still livid and, quite literally in the case of many of their subjects, ran deep. The mandarins of the F.O., it appeared, were unwilling to rub salt into them.

It fell to Mr. R. L. Speight to sound the first note of caution on 26th July. Whilst he concurred with the proposal to approach the

14

Political Intelligence Department for a composite response, he was concerned that, 'Mr. Masefield asks for a lot and I do not know if we can give him all he requires. The W[ar] O[ffice] will have to be contacted about A & B, & I imagine that we should want to vet the book before publication.' He concluded by wondering whether, as a first step, '. . . P.I.D. would let us have some idea of what they would propose to produce for Mr. Masefield.'[12]

A response was minuted the following day by Mr. C. P. A. Warner, who informed Mr. Speight that a general reply to B could be furnished, '. . . from the November crisis onwards', but questioned whether any details could be given, '. . . without the approval of the Dutch and Belgian governments'. There were also concerns about what exactly Masefield had meant with regard to the Belgian King Leopold's 'words of regret and extenuation' for his surrender. Now the ball was well and truly rolling as others chimed in with their misgivings.

On 31st July Mr. Lambert added an extensive minute endorsing Mr Warner's comments but examining Masefield's request for clarification of the nature of the refusals of Holland and Belgium to consider Staff Talks before the German invasion in greater detail. 'B presents rather a delicate problem' Lambert began, ' If the line is taken that the Allies pressed the Belgians to engage in staff talks and were rebuffed by the latter, this might provide an opening for German propaganda in Belgium to say "we told you so. The Allies were trying all the time to drag you into their military machine." Any reference to this question would have to be carefully worded, and I think we should vet the text.'[13] The paper found its way back to Mr. Warr who, on 2nd August, suggested that it might be returned to P.I.D. so that they could '. . . compose a memorandum' which they could see before it was sent to Masefield.

There now followed a delay of eight days until Mr. Speight responded on 10th August. He felt sure that the Foreign Office could satisfy Masefield on his points D, E and F by showing him the relevant dispatches from Brussels, Poitiers and the Hague. On point C, he felt that they could explain that scrutiny of their archives was unnecessary and that Masefield should be referred to the Chatham House Organization at Balliol College, which would probably have the relevant information on file. That left the thorny issue of points A and B.

It was at this point that the possibility of referring the issue to a higher authority was raised. 'A & B are the real snags. We might ask Gen. Ismay what we can say about A. & get the P.I.D. to prepare something on B. which we could submit to Gen. Ismay & the W.O. for approval.' Speight was adamant that 'the difficulties which these points raise' should be spelled out to Masefield.

A week later Sir Stephen Gaselee composed a suitable response to Masefield based on the accumulated observations but nevertheless invited the Poet Laureate to make an appointment to visit the Foreign Office library.

Although there were serious concerns regarding the substance of the information to be released to Masefield and the style of its presentation, up to this point no-one had questioned the wisdom of publishing such a work much less Masefield's right to do it. After all hadn't he been 'asked' to write it? Hadn't he received Churchill's blessing? On the same day that Sir Stephen Gaselee wrote to Masefield, another letter was sent from the Foreign Office to Major General Ismay at the War Cabinet Office to which was attached Masefield's original letter of 24th July.[14] From this point onward questions began to be raised which cast doubt on the veracity of Masefield's claim that he had been 'asked' to write a book. It was also the first hint that some form of official statement or publication should be released in order to counter any claims of being 'left in the lurch' which might be made by a rancorous French government now exhibiting a marked Anglophobe complexion.

Dear Ismay,

I enclose a copy of the letter which Gaselee, our Librarian, has received from the Poet Laureate asking for information on certain points in connexion with a book which he is writing on the Belgian campaign. I understand that the project was originally referred by Mr. Masefield to the Prime Minister who generally approved it and referred the Poet Laureate to the Ministry of Information and the War Office for practical assistance. Colonel Neville is dealing with the matter at the Ministry of Information where he acts as liaison with the War Office.

2. Points (c), (d), (e) and (f) . . . do not present any great difficulty. Point (c) can be largely answered from public sources,

and we are proposing to let him read despatches from our representatives at Brussels and The Hague which should give him what he wants on (d), (e) and (f).

3. Points (a) and (b) about our military obligations to France and our efforts to initiate staff conversations with Holland and Belgium present a more awkward problem. The Foreign Office are not competent to express an opinion as to how much information may be made public on these subjects and we must invoke the assistance of the War Cabinet Offices. Apart from Mr. Masefield's enquiry it would be useful for our own purposes to prepare a statement – in particular on the question of our promise of military support for France. We have not overlooked the Secretary of State for War's statement in Parliament on the 6th August that it is not yet desirable to publish an account of our military operations, but we think that something should be got ready for publication in order to refute any misleading statements about the part we played which the Petain Government may put out in the course of the Riom trials.[15] Such an account might usefully be illustrated by quotations from official documents, possibly even from the minutes of the Supreme War Council (which are in any case presumably in German hands by now). It also seems important to select the extracts in such a way as to bring out the point that the brunt of the operations before May 10th were borne by the British Navy and Air Force and that all offensive action against Germany was persistently blocked by the French High Command. This document, when prepared, could be shown to Mr. Masefield as background, and published later if necessary.

4. We should be grateful for your comments on this proposal, and, if you agree to it, for any suggestions as to how we should proceed with the compilation of the document. We have already put Woodward, the Oxford historian, who works in the Political Intelligence Department on to producing a document to refute the accusation that we dragged the French into the war last September by refusing the Italian suggestion for a conference. Possibly he might be brought in to help with the compilation of the other document also.

Yours ever
(Sd). O.G. Sargent.[16]

17

Masefield visited the Foreign Office on the afternoon of 26th August and in spite of a forty minute delay due to an air raid warning, he managed to work his way through five files, dictating notes as he went to Miss Sullivan, a shorthand typist on loan to him for the afternoon. Miss Sullivan typed the notes up 'beautifully' according to Masefield who acknowledged their receipt on 29th August. During Masefield's visit, Sir Stephen Gaselee had gleaned a little more about the origin of the idea for his book.

'I ascertained' wrote Sir Stephen on 28th August, 'that this projected history of the Flanders Campaign was initiated by the Poet Laureate, *proprio motu*, in a letter to the Prime Minister, who apparently accepted it with enthusiasm: but I don't think that anything was said about it to us from No. 10. I first heard of it as the result of a letter from the Poet Laureate to Sir Robert Vansittart.' It was now becoming clear that Masefield had not been 'asked' to write a book at all.

The reply to Sir Orme Sargent's letter to General Ismay at the War Cabinet Office, written on Ismay's behalf by Colonel Hollis, one of Ismay's lieutenants, prompted a call for further investigations into who exactly gave Masefield permission to embark on his book. It is entirely possible that when Ismay asked Hollis to respond to the Foreign Office, Churchill's minute of 19th July, issued to ensure that his name was not 'used loosely', was still ringing in his ears.

> Prime Minister to General Ismay, C.I.G.S., and Sir Edward Bridges
> Let it be very clearly understood that all directions emanating from me are made in writing, or should be immediately afterwards confirmed in writing, and that I do not accept any responsibility for matters relating to national defence on which I am alleged to have given a decision unless they are recorded in writing.[17]

Thus, after confirming that he was collecting together documents about Britain's military obligations to France and the Staff Conversations with Holland and Belgium, together with a warning that he had not the staff to go through the vast quantities of papers to produce an answer '. . . in the form that Mr. Masefield would like', Colonel Hollis concluded, 'I think it would be just worth while checking up on the question of how far the Prime Minister did, in fact, authorise Mr. Masefield to call upon Departments for information. Naturally if he has received the full authority of the Prime Minister, there is nothing more to be said.'[18] But there was more, much more, to be said. Highlighting the last paragraph of Hollis's letter, Sir Orme Sargent wrote, 'Please find out from No 10' and passed it on. The paper landed on the desk of Mr. F. K. Roberts, who minuted his findings on 6th September.

I have had some difficulty checking up the point raised in the last paragraph of this letter. Mr. Roger Stevens, who had provided me with the information summarised in our letter to General Ismay, confessed that he had only received it secondhand, and as a result of further conversations with Col. Neville, the War Office representative of the M.o.I., and Mr. Russell, the Private Secretary, [in the Ministry of Information] I have ascertained that the position is as follows:-

Mr. Masefield originally sent a telegram to the Prime Minister saying he would like to write a history of the Flanders Campaign, similar to his history of the Gallipoli campaign. The Prime Minister referred this telegram to the War Office, without however actually expressing any opinion. The War Office and the Ministry of Information assumed that he had approved it and I gather there is no reason to suppose that he did not. Meanwhile Mr. Masefield has been given the facilities required and is in close touch with the Minister of Information [Alfred Duff Cooper] himself who has certainly given his official approval to the project, as have the War Office. The Ministry of Information were quite satisfied that it was unnecessary to refer the matter back again to the Prime Minister, so I have not risked starting an unnecessary 'hare' by speaking to anybody at No. 10.

The Ministry had informed Roberts that Masefield's book was already 'well under way' but that it would not be as near complete an account as the one the Foreign Office were planning to collate. Roberts suggested that the best course of action would be to regard Masefield's book as quite separate from the 'more detailed research which we shall ourselves require Mr. Woodward to do.'[19]

Meanwhile Mr. Oliver Harvey of the Ministry of Information had telephoned Roberts to say that he was keen to publish an official response to possible 'French misrepresentations', more specifically allegations centred on the lack of British military support for France made by a French Cabinet Minister, M. Paul Baudouin.[20] Roberts promised to confirm by letter the Foreign Office's position regarding an answer to Baudouin's claims that was duly written on 9th September, a similar draft of which went to Colonel Hollis at the War Cabinet Office. It appeared that the Poet Laureate's request had rattled more than one government cage.

Roberts explained to Harvey that the issue of the French allegations had first surfaced in early August in connection with the Riom Trials and at that stage the Foreign Office had proposed getting in touch with the War Cabinet Office with a view to collecting the material necessary for a reply. It was only then that the Foreign Office had learned that Masefield had been in touch with the Ministry of Information and the War Office and that Masefield had been allowed access to certain documents at the Ministry of Information as well as those in their own library. There was no doubt that his book, according to Roberts, was 'already on the stocks'. That said the Foreign Office was keen to liaise with the War Cabinet Office so that their historical expert, Professor Woodward, could prepare '. . . a more carefully documented study [of Britain's military obligations to France] than Masefield's book is likely to provide'.

On the same day, Mr. William Strang, another Foreign Office official, put his name to the draft sent to Colonel Hollis in reply to his letter of 31st August to Sir Orme Sargent, in which Hollis had raised questions about who had given approval for Masefield's book. It was couched in terms almost identical to those expressed by Mr. Roberts in his letter to Mr. Harvey.

When Professor Woodward, the Foreign Office's historian, eventually made contact with Colonel Hollis to discuss the issue of the compilation of a 'complete and documented account' of the campaign, it transpired that someone in the War Cabinet Office had somehow come to the same conclusion and that they were embarking on the same course of action. Hollis told the Oxford Don in no uncertain terms that, '. . . any outside intervention would not be welcome' and that Colonel Yule was now engaged on the task. Was the War Cabinet Office closing ranks and protecting its own interests? 'Outside intervention' presumably applied to anyone not

20

supported by the War Cabinet Office and that would certainly have included Masefield as well as the Foreign Office's chosen man.

This new stance of the War Cabinet Office came as rather a surprise to the Foreign Office and particularly Mr. Roberts, who remarked that it had been Hollis who had earlier requested that they should 'provide the historian'. 'I think we must avoid being short-circuited on this important political issue', wrote Roberts on 12th September. It was turning out to be a right old Whitehall muddle.

Masefield was apparently oblivious to the questions, the flow of ink and the sheaves of headed paper his project was generating in government. Indeed, he had no reason to suspect anything unto-ward as he continued to receive a steady stream of help from an apparently cooperative Foreign Office. On 10th September Sir Stephen Gaselee had furnished him with a response to his additional queries regarding the numbers of Belgian and Dutch ships sunk and seamen drowned prior to the German invasion. Gaselee had obtained the information from the respective Missions in London. The figures, Masefield said, would be used 'with much discretion'. But the drama still had some months left to run and there was an explosive twist left in store for the denouement.

Masefield obviously wrote like fury during that autumn of 1940. At the beginning of October, Heinemann, his publisher, asked that the typescript be sent 'as soon as it is finished' and at that point, according to research carried out by Dr. Philip W. Errington, the present archivist of the John Masefield Society, there was some discussion as to whether to set the material as soon as it came in or wait until it had been passed. Less than three months after Masefield had sent his original letter to Sir Stephen Gaselee the typescript was complete. Like Masefield's book on Gallipoli, too little time had passed since the events of which he wrote had occurred for his book to be a complete history but it was a history nevertheless; a history which, while recording a military defeat, celebrated a 'victory' of the spirit, of freedom and democracy over dark forces of evil. It was a history that Masefield hoped would cross the Atlantic, as had been the case with his *Gallipoli*, to open the eyes of America to the tyranny and oppression he believed had enveloped Europe.

Heinemann acknowledged receipt of the typescript on 11th October and it appears as though it was set as soon as it was received. It was duly passed to the Ministry of Information, whose

Chief Press Censor received it on 25th October, scrutinized it and informed Masefield on 9th November that his book had 'now been vetted by the necessary authorities and passed from the security point of view'. Eleven days later Heinemann sent a package to Masefield which contained 'a couple of proofs in book form of THE TWENTY FIVE DAYS',[21] asking him to check the text, correct it and pass it ready for the press. Masefield was obviously refining and adding new material all the time for on 25th November C.S. Evans wrote to thank him for sending the '. . . verses to go at the end of THE TWENTY FIVE DAYS'.

A little over a week later events took a drastic turn for the worse when the existence of the work, by now well and truly set and with proofs in book form, came to the attention of Anthony Eden, the Secretary of State for War.

Just after Christmas, on 28th December, Mr. T. Cash at the War Office rang Mr. J. H. E. Woods at the Treasury regarding a most important, yet delicate matter. He confirmed their telephone conversation in a letter marked <u>SECRET</u> that left Whitehall, Treasury bound, that same afternoon. Its contents were dynamite.

Dear Woods,

I spoke to you this afternoon about the question of John Masefield's book "Twentyfive days".

The history of the matter is that three or four months ago Mr. Masefield asked the Prime Minister if he might be supplied with material for a narrative of the battle of Flanders and the retreat to Dunkirk. The Prime Minister gave permission and material was supplied through the Ministry of Information and this office . . . the Secretary of State for War (Mr. Eden) first heard about the book on the 4th December and gave instructions immediately for the book to be re-examined in order that it might be ascertained that no passages in it would lead to a demand for the publication of the despatches or of any other official documents relating to the withdrawal. The book was accordingly read by Sir Edward Grigg, who advised that in his opinion, from the policy point of view, publication would be disastrous, the general impression left, so far as the Army was concerned, being one of general chaos redeemed by occasional gleams of individual bravery, but otherwise putting both the Army and its leadership in a very poor light. [22]

Mr. Eden wrote to the Prime Minister on the 20th December saying that he felt very unhappy as to the effect which such a publication was likely to produce, both here and in the United States, but that the situation was complicated by the fact that the publishers in both countries already have the book in page proof and that Mr. Masefield is pressing strongly for its release by us. He went on to say that he felt that the only way out was for someone to tell Masefield that he must re-write the book under 'guidance' and obviously that someone must be the Prime Minister or somebody with his full authority. He, (Mr. Eden) certainly could not willingly see published a book which assessed at their full value the services of the Navy and the R.A.F. at Dunkirk, while making of the operations which preceded it, nothing but a succession of isolated minor incidents unconnected with any plan or any purpose.

The Prime Minister's instructions to the Secretary of State are **"You should veto the publication and induce or compel Mr. Masefield to recast his story so as to meet the points you have in mind. We are entitled to do this as he asked for special facilities which were granted to him. You have my full authority to proceed on these lines."** (My emphasis.)

A letter to Mr. Masefield has been drafted accordingly, but it is considered that it is necessary to include in it a statement that Masefield's publishers, both here and in the United States, and Masefield himself will be given reasonable compensation for the actual expenses to which they have been, or may be put, in breaking and resetting type, advance publicity etc, We do not propose to make any effort to compensate for loss of profits though it is, of course, not unlikely that a claim for that will follow.

The despatch of this letter is regarded here as a matter of great urgency in view of the pressure which Mr. Masefield and his publishers have been exerting for some time for a decision. I appreciate your difficulty in dealing with a point of this importance over the telephone but I should be very grateful if you could let me know as soon as possible after receiving this, whether you agree that we may put such a promise to meet expenses in the letter. We cannot, I am afraid, at this stage, give any indication of the amount.[23]

Now the Treasury was involved and there was no doubt that the wrangling, the misunderstandings and the false assumptions over the book had eventually embroiled Churchill himself. Heinemann had already caught a whiff of official reluctance and C. S. Evans may have already begun to realize that permission to publish may not now be granted. He wrote to Masefield on 11th December, citing the British Commander-in-Chief as one of the possible reasons behind the blocking of the book. There were suggestions, he said, that 'Gort himself may want to write a book on the same subject which could not be published until after the war and is afraid that you may have stolen some of his thunder'.[24] This would be entirely consistent with a desire by Gort, still smarting over the publicity accorded his Army during the campaign and perhaps worried that the Navy and R.A.F. had 'had a better show', to write his own memoir and thus set the record straight.

Mr. Cash's letter was now circulated to officials in the Treasury and before Mr. Woods drafted his reply Mr. C.H.M. Wilcox shared his thoughts. Whilst conceding that the Treasury would have to support the War Office's stance, his comments, written on 30th December, reveal that he was not unsympathetic to Masefield's position.

Mr Woods.

I think we shall have to agree to the War Office proposal to reimburse Mr Masefield for actual expenses incurred through the rewriting of his book. It is true that he would not have been able to write the book without the official material supplied to him, but once he had been given the 'all clear' by the Director of Public Relations he was entitled to assume that there would be no further hold-up by the authorities.

I imagine that it will not be easy to get Mr Masefield to rewrite his book in any case, and he would have it in his power to make the authorities look very foolish.

In any case he will have them re the hold up as with each week that passes Dunkirk loses some of its topicality.[25]

On the last day of 1940 the Treasury officially acquiesced to the War Office's proposal and Mr. Woods authorized reimbursement in a brief letter, the final paragraph of which provides a delightful example of an attempt at damage limitation in pure Treasury speak.

> Dear Cash,
> In reply to your letter of the 28th December about the Masefield book, we agree that in the rather unfortunate circumstances it is inevitable that you should give some indication to Masefield that he and his publishers both here and in the United States will be given reasonable compensation for any actual expenses to which they may be, or have been put, in breaking and re-setting the type etc.
> The 'etc.' is rather difficult and no doubt you will do your best to confine the undertaking within the narrowest possible limits.[26]

That, it appeared, was that. Masefield had once again fallen victim to official censorship for reasons of 'security'. All that was left was to inform Masefield and at the beginning of January 1941, he appears to have communicated the bad news to Heinemann, while at the same time, requesting that before the typeset was broken, Heinemann make up twenty-five proof copies in book form, which would at least contain the new material sent after the initial proofs in book form had been produced in late November the previous year. There were now in existence, in book proof form, two versions of *The Twenty-Five Days*, dated 1940 and 1941. These two proofs show the text in different states. 'The 1940 proof includes small sections that were later re -written or omitted from the 1941 version. Within the 1940 proof there are five maps, as in the 1941 proof, but the page listing, headed 'Maps and Illustrations' in 1941 is merely headed 'Illustrations' in 1940. There are also changes to the setting of text and the half-title, title-page and running titles (which read 'THE TWENTYFIVE DAYS' in 1940 and 'THE TWENTY-FIVE DAYS' in 1941). The 1941 proof includes seven poems not present in 1940.[27] These are:

(Untitled) 'They marched over the Field of Waterloo'
(Untitled) 'In the black Maytime when we faced the worst'
(Untitled) 'When someone somewhere bids the bombing cease'
(Untitled) 'Not any drums or bugles with Last Post'
(Untitled) 'O smiling, sun-burned youth who rode the sky'
(Untitled) 'Let a people reading stories full of anguish'

(Untitled) 'Ah, when the spirit knows the dewy dawn, the peace time'

It was the 1941 proof which, with its additional material, was the one that Masefield felt was nearer to his ideal of a finished work and the one that he and his publisher had obviously intended to produce.

Within days of the suppression of the book the possibility of salvaging something from the project was being discussed. There is no evidence to suggest that Masefield even considered a re-write. From his aborted commission to write a book on the battle of the Somme in 1917-18, Masefield had at least salvaged *The Old Front Line*. Now he was intent on trying to do the same with *The Twenty-Five Days*. Had he not already written in *The Twenty-Five Days* that, '. . . Dunquerque (*sic*) had been a nine days' wonder needing a story to itself' and had then gone on to tell the story, day by day, of the evacuation? Why not turn this section into a book in its own right? There were also other pressures that may have hastened Masefield's desire to publish part of his work. During March 1941, Heinemann informed Masefield that '. . . a book on the Dunkirk evacuation by Lord Gort has been announced'. *The Nine Days Wonder* – a work often compared with Masefield's *Gallipoli* – was subsequently published in April 1941. Masefield, ever the story-teller, dedicated 'this tale' to 'Vice Admiral Bertram Ramsay, K.C.B., M.V.O' and 'The Officers, Warrant-Officers and ratings, and to all others who bore a hand in the operation Dynamo'. It was a dedication not present in either the 1940 or 1941 proof copies of *The Twenty-Five Days*. Masefield also added further material, as there are poems that appear in *The Nine Days Wonder* which are not present in either the 1940 or 1941 proof versions. Only four of the 1941 verses appear in *The Nine Days Wonder* by which time three had acquired titles:

(Untitled) 'They marched over the Field of Waterloo'

Thoughts for Later On 'When someone somewhere bids the bombing cease'

A Young English Air-Man 'O smiling, sun-burned youth who rode the sky'

When We Return Thanks 'Ah, when the spirit knows the dewy dawn, the peace time'

Even in the case of this salvaged work, there are published copies which also show the text in different states. During his research for

The Twenty-Five Days, Masefield had interviewed five small craft skippers who had played a prominent role in the evacuation from Dunkirk. All had received the Distinguished Service Medal for their actions but the exploits of only one of them, Able Seaman Samuel Parker, the skipper of the *Naiad Errant,* had been granted half a page by the Poet Laureate. When John Richards became a joint owner of this famous 'Little Ship' he purchased a second copy of *The Nine Days Wonder* in case he might some day loan one and never see it again. It was while Richards was checking both copies for his book on the *Naiad Errant,* that he found variations in the text, although both had been printed in April 1941. Richards was puzzled. 'Why had Masefield altered the entry about my boat when a thorough search through both books revealed to me no other changes'? A comparison . . . indicated the cause. Masefield had originally included the words,

she was rushed and swamped by French soldiers

This was changed to,

she was unfortunately swamped and washed ashore.

The second change replaced the last sentence with,

This boat helped save the crew of the French destroyer *Sirocco* when sinking off the port.[28]

'Swamping' was, and remains today, a very potent and politically emotive term. The reference to being 'swamped by French soldiers' is present in both the 1940 and 1941 proofs of *The Twenty-Five Days*. Richards concluded that because both changes in his two copies of *The Nine Days Wonder* concerned the French, the first amendment deleted a negative reference to them whilst the second inserted a positive reference to the British in relation to them. He postulated that Masefield must have been under pressure to delete the negative reference about the French 'swamping my boat'. It is entirely possible that Masefield made those amendments as a result of the letter from the War Office early in 1941.

Masefield was obviously anxious that Heinemann recover the

costs of the aborted project and by 29th May it appeared that recompense had indeed been made as C.S. Evans reported, in a letter that day, that '. . . we have received payment from the War Office in connection with THE TWENTY-FIVE DAYS'. To date no evidence of the exact figure paid to Heinemann has come to light.

And there the story of *The Twenty-Five Days* rested for thirty years until 1972 when Heinemann, in association with the Society of Authors, acting for the Executors of the Masefield Estate, finally published an edition of his work. A publisher's note, informed readers that, at last, clearance had been obtained from the Ministry of Defence, 'to publish the whole account, which includes the section published as *The Nine Days Wonder* but in its original, fuller form' and that they wished to 'acknowledge the role of Mr. Alan Smith of the Conway Maritime Press in the production of the book'. Also recorded were thanks due to Miss Diana Daniels for her help and cooperation.[29]

Research carried out by Dr. Philip W. Errington revealed that the Conway Maritime Press evidently intended to publish the volume during the 1970s, Diana Daniels having mentioned the existence of the title after assisting with the Conway Maritime Press 1971 edition of *Sea Life in Nelson's Time*. In November 1971, after making an approach to the Society of Authors, the Conway Maritime Press consulted Heinemann to establish their claim to the work. By the following month Heinemann had evidently decided to publish the volume themselves for they initiated a search to find a copy of the text. Miss Diana Daniels owned a proof copy in her private collection and assisted Heinemann by providing a line by line typescript in which she admitted to correcting 'obvious typographical errors'. Dr. Errington, however, found that Miss Daniels harboured reservations about the project as she stated that the publication of the Heinemann volume would significantly diminish the commercial value of her proof copy.[30]

Errington's research confirmed that Miss Daniels had worked from a 1940 proof copy to create the typescript for the 1972 publication and that the existence of proof copies dating from 1941 was unknown in 1972. That said there are significant differences between the 1972 text and the 1940 proof from which it was fashioned.

It has already been noted that amendments had been made to later editions of *The Nine Days Wonder* with the excision of controversial text in some cases and the addition of more favourable passages in others. The first edition of *The Nine Days Wonder* held by the British Library is different from the section on Dunkirk in both the 1940 and 1941 proofs. It cannot therefore, be in its 'original and fuller form'.

The clear sections that are present in the 1940 proof are less well defined in 1972 and the 1972 typesetting is also much tighter and more compact. Masefield's original spelling of 'Dunquerque' is anglicized to the more familiar 'Dunkirk' and his rather archaic use of 'shewn', still in use in 1940 but almost extinct by 1972, is replaced by 'shown'. The dedication to Vice Admiral Sir Bertram Ramsay and the Officers, Warrant Officers and all others who took part in Operation Dynamo was never a part of the original work, being absent in the 1940 proof, but it is identical to that in *The Nine Days Wonder*. Further evidence to support the thesis that the 1972 publication was based on a 1940 proof centres on the additional material in the form of the poems which Masefield sent to Heinemann after the 1940 proofs had been printed. There are no poems in the 1972 edition.

In addition to the above, there are also differences between the 1972 text and that of the 1941 proof. There are certain typographical differences – a hyphen dropped here, a capital letter added there, and conventions regarding the writing of dates are altered – but specific textual variations have much more far reaching implications. On page 1 of the 1941 proof, Masefield had written about how British governments during the inter-war years had strived to maintain peace abroad and improve the nation at home. The laying of the foundations of a 'new and splendid nation' was, he felt, a thanksgiving for Britain's deliverance – a word almost certainly selected intentionally as Dunkirk was also hailed as a deliverance – from the nightmare of the Great War. 'It was' he wrote '. . . a showing of our gratitude to the million of our race whose lives were lost in that disaster.'[31] In the 1972 publication the word 'million' becomes 'millions'. This is very significant indeed for it is a corruption of reality that has helped to cloud objective study of the First World War over the years. 740,000 British soldiers were killed during the First World War with a further 170,000 Empire and Dominions dead giving a total of 910,000.

Not quite a million, certainly not 'millions'. Masefield was nearer the mark than those who had a hand in preparing the 1972 volume for print and the additional 's' is significant because it might have contributed to an orthodoxy and the development of a myth which became established during the 1960s and carried through into the 1970s, of a futile war in which 'millions' of British soldiers lost their lives. True, a figure of 910,000 dead is staggering and British commanders made some spectacular errors of judgement that led to dreadful numbers of casualties but 'millions' of Britons did not die. It is a myth, still peddled today and which many Britons still believe.

Given the year of its publication it is easy to understand why that extra 's' might have slipped into the 1972 volume of *The Twenty-Five Days* for greater impact, but Masefield did not mean 'millions' and he certainly did not write it in 1941. Elsewhere an 's' has been deleted from Masefield's original text as is the case when he makes reference to the French General Georges 'groups' of Northern Armies.[32]

The maps in the 1941 proof are reproduced from official maps – they bear references – whereas the 1972 maps appear to have been redrawn by George Hartfield Limited.

Now, more than thirty years on from that 1972 edition, interest in the 1940 campaign has still not faded. On the contrary, it appears as though it is as topical today as it was more than sixty years ago. At the time of writing the BBC has just completed its screening of a major, three-part docudrama on Dunkirk, produced at vast expense, and received with wide critical acclaim. The public's appetite for programmes, books and articles on the 1940 campaign and the story of the 'salvation' of the British Army at Dunkirk appears undiminished and is still being fed by major publishers. Putting 'Dunkirk' in the title of a book on the 1940 campaign still helps to shift more copies than if it were omitted.

What better time then to publish an account of that campaign by a man who cared passionately for his country, served his country and still felt that Britain's armed forces of 1940, albeit eye deep in yet another 'last ditch', as had so often been the case in the past, could still produce real heroes? What better time to produce a version of an account of that campaign never before seen in its original form? What better time to publish *The Twenty-Five Days*, the book John Masefield always intended and the book that Churchill's government did not want you to read?

Notes

1. William Buchan (ed.) *John Masefield – Letters to Reyna* (London: Buchan and Enright, 1983) p. 26.
2. Melvyn Bragg, *The Adventure of English – The Biography of a Language* (London: Hodder and Stoughton, 2003) p.8.
3. *Ibid.* p. 35.
4. Peter Vansittart, (ed.) *John Masefield's Letters from the Front 1915–17* (London: Constable and Co., 1984) p.36.
5. John Masefield, *The Twenty Five Days* 1941 proof copy. The British Library. X.708/8995.
6. Vansittart *op.cit.* p.31.
7. Dr. Philip W. Errington, *John Masefield –The 'Great Auk' of English Literature – A Bibliography*, (London: The British Library 2004) p.556.
8. Constance Babington Smith, *John Masefield – A Life* (New York: Macmillan, 1978) p.163.
9. *Ibid.* p.166.
10. The National Archives, FO 371/24424.
11. Ian Ousby, *Occupation – The Ordeal of France 1940 –1944* (London: Pimlico, 1999) p.p. 36–42.
12. The National Archives, FO 371/24424.
13. *Ibid.*
14. Major General Hastings Lionel Ismay had been head of the pre-war Secretariat of the Committee of Imperial Defence. When Winston Churchill became Prime Minister on 10th May, he also absorbed the office of Minister of Defence into his duties and Ismay became his Chief of Staff. Ismay's principal lieutenants at the Ministry of Defence were Colonels Hollis and Jacob to whom Churchill paid tribute in the second volume of his *The Second World War*. Churchill trusted Ismay, who also held the post of Deputy Secretary (Military) of the War Cabinet, implicitly, so much so that Ismay later remarked that he had spent 'the whole war in the middle of the web'. Interestingly, for a story which involved the War Cabinet Office and the Poet Laureate, Ismay's direct superior as Secretary of the War Cabinet was Sir Edward Bridges, son of the poet Robert Bridges, John Masefield's immediate predecessor.
15. The Riom trial, named after the town of Riom near Vichy, eventually began to hear indictments against some of the most senior politicians in France in the spring of 1941. It was the Vichy regime's attempt to

stage a 'show trial' to investigate the origins of the French defeat in 1940 but it collapsed in disarray after some of the 'accused' managed to mount such a strong defence of their actions that they caused acute embarrassment to the Petain government.

16 The National Archives, FO 371/24424.
17 Winston S. Churchill, *The Second World War. Vol. II. – Their Finest Hour* (London: Cassell, 1949) p.17.
18 The National Archives, FO 371/24424.
19 *Ibid.*
20 Paul Baudouin, a long time advocate of an armistice with Germany, became one of the leading doves in the French cabinet after his promotion in M. Reynaud's cabinet reshuffle of 5th June 1940.
21 Errington, *op.cit.* p.557.
22 It is clear, from documents in the National Archive, that Lord Gort, Commander-in-Chief of the Army at the time of the retreat and evacuation, was extremely dissatisfied with the publicity given to the Field Force during the campaign and, in late June 1940, actually tore a strip off the members of the P.R. Department and particularly its Overseas Unit, for being 'extremely inefficient'. This provoked a spirited rebuttal from the P.R. Department, which compiled a lengthy report detailing, amongst other things, the exact numbers of photographs taken, newsreels shot and the arrangements made for war correspondents to interview returning troops. See The National Archives WO 258/10
23 The National Archives, T 161/1003
24 Errington, *op.cit.* p.557.
25 The National Archives, T161/1003
26 *Ibid.*
27 Errington, *op.cit.* p.558.
28 John Richards, John Masefield, Dunkirk And My Boat *The Journal of the John Masefield Society*, Vol. 10, May 2001. pp. 38 – 40. See also John Richards, *Your Now Famous Motor Boat – The Story of John Masefield and the* Naiad Errant (Shepperton: Naiad Errant Archive Publications)
29 John Masefield, *The Twenty-Five Days* (London: William Heinemann Ltd. 1972) p.vi.
30 Errington, *op.cit.*
31 John Masefield, *The Twenty Five Days* 1941 proof copy. The British Library. X.708/8995.
32 *Ibid.*, p.4.

THE
TWENTY-FIVE
DAYS

They marched over the Field of Waterloo,
By Gomont and La Haie, and then fell back,
Forever facing front to the attack
Across the English bones.

Westward, by Fontenoy, their ranks withdrew;
The German many bomb-bursts beat the drum;
And many a trooper marched to kingdom come
Upon the Flanders stones.

Westward they went, past Wipers and the old
Fields bought and paid for by their brothers' blood.
Their feet were in the snapping of the flood
That sped to gulf them down.

They were as bridegrooms plighted to the mould,
Those marching men with neither hope nor star:
The German in the gateways as a bar,
The sea beyond to drown.

And at the very sea, a cloud of night,
A hail of death and allies in collapse;
A foe in the perfection of his traps;
A certainty of doom.

When, lo, out of the darkness there was light,
There in the sea were England and her ships:
They sailed with the free salt upon their lips
To sunlight from the tomb.

PREFACE

THIS is the story of an advance followed by a long retreat and withdrawal in difficult conditions. Probably no single soldier in the B.E.F. thought or thinks of the campaign as a defeat. The men of the B.E.F. knew from experience, that man for man they were better than the enemy. Three weeks of desperate fighting had shewn them that the enemy's success was due to great numbers of machines, aeroplanes, tanks and guns.

Our men knew, too, that the enemy had profited by extraordinary miscalculations, for which not one of them was in any way responsible. As a part of an Allied Army Group, they had been ordered forward to attack. They had hardly reached the attacking positions before the Army on their left flank was gravely compromised, and the Army on their right flank threatened. Three days later, the Army on their left flank was falling back and the Army on their right flank was broken through. At once, the B.E.F. found itself with its right flank turned, its left flank in danger, and its communications imperilled. It was in the most dangerous position that the war offered. Those who had imperilled it had foreseen nothing of the kind and were unable to improvise measures to kill the danger. There was nothing for it but to fall back, and falling back was made almost impossible from the first by the multitudes of refugees on the roads. Our men could only crawl back, while the enemy raced to cut them from the sea. By the foresight of Lord Gort, makeshift guards to the flanks were improvised instantly. It was due to his foresight and the extraordinary self-sacrificing valour of these guards that the enemy's plan to encircle and annihilate three Allied Armies was ruined.

The withdrawal of the B.E.F. from a position of extreme danger, with flanks in peril, communications almost gone, and the enemy above and in front was achieved by wisdom in the leader and heroism in the men.

To all who took part in this adventure, I dedicate this tale.

JOHN MASEFIELD.

BETWEEN the years 1919 and 1938 our Governments strove to preserve peace abroad and to improve the nation at home. In the second of these tasks, they met with little opposition. The last war had shown how great the need for improvement was. Their success, in the improvement of all ways and standards of life, in the lifting of barriers, in the changing for the better all ancient concepts of Citizen and State, was outstanding and such as had never yet been seen. It was so great that those who remembered what had been in the late nineteenth and in the first years of the twentieth century, could only marvel at the miracle.

This laying of the foundations of a new and splendid nation, was in part a thanksgiving for our deliverance from the nightmare of the Great War. It was in part a showing of our gratitude to the million of our race whose lives were lost in that disaster.

When the Great War ended, many peoples hoped that war would not again disgrace and ruin humanity. They helped to found and establish a League of Nations, which served mankind ably, until defections made it no longer a League. Even when this hope of man had failed to stop or check wars of aggression, this country continued to work for peace, believing that one modern war was sufficient abomination for one era.

Others thought otherwise. The revolutionary governments in Italy and Germany began to apply to nations the methods by which they had overcome opposing cliques.

The repeated acts of aggression by Italy and Germany are fresh in memory. The abominations began with Italy's invasion of Abyssinia in 1935. This was followed in 1936 by Germany's re-occupation of the Rhineland, in defiance of the Locarno Treaties. During the joint adventure of Italy and Germany in Spain, Germany, by craft and brutality, prepared and carried through her attacks upon Austria and Czechoslovakia. After this, by her attack upon Poland on September the 1st, 1939, she compelled France and Great Britain to declare war upon her.

In the first nine months of the war we sent to France 422,000 men, with their guns, transport, stores, repair-shops, ammunition, medical supplies and hospitals, with all their maintenance of every kind. We made their tents, huts, camps and aerodromes; we organised their lines of supply, their water-points and fuel-stations, and this, in one of the severest winters known in Europe.

No other nation in history has sent so great a force overseas in so short a time. The efforts necessary in any such shipment are enormous. All things used and needed by such an army have to be gathered, packed and entrained to a port, loaded in ships, sailed to a port, unloaded, put into some sort of a supply-train, and sent by road or rail to some dump or rail-head. There they are unloaded, sorted out and carried to those who use them. This fourfold or five-fold effort was made with each man and thing sent to France. In the shifting of nearly a million tons of goods four or five times, a vast power of labour is used. The shifting of this weight of supply was but a part of the effort necessary. In some parts of the process, the facts of war doubled the difficulties; the long supply-train was made longer, and being longer had to be carefully guarded. In peace, France can be reached by ship in little more than an hour. In time of war, the seas are mined, and the channels made tortuous. Each man and thing sent goes under the guard of warships by the constant toil of the mine-sweepers and the vigilance of air-patrols. Let those who blame us for this or that reflect on these things. Let them remember that the men and things sent were sent across waters within a day's steam and ninety minutes' flight of an enemy bent on their destruction, and that of all those men and tons of things neither man nor thing was lost by enemy action on the way. Let them remember, also, that no nation can strip her shores of defenders. With a long coastline, containing hundreds of miles of beach on which enemy landing is possible, this nation must expect and guard against invasion or a succession of raids: she cannot send all her defenders, guns, tanks and aeroplanes abroad.

Our army in France was known as the British Expeditionary Force, usually abbreviated to the B.E.F.

It was under the command of the French Commander-in-Chief, the General Gamelin, whose strategical aim governed its action.

The groups of Northern Armies, with which the B.E.F. was associated, was under the command of General Alphonse Joseph Georges.

General Marie Gustave Gamelin, then sixty-two years of age, was a practised and famous soldier. As a boy, he had shown promise as a painter, but chose the Army as his profession. After serving some years in Africa, he entered the Ecole de Guerre, where Marshal Foch was then Professor of Tactics. Later, he commanded a battalion of the Corps d'Elite, the Chasseurs Alpins. In 1906, he was on the Staff of General Joffre, then a divisional General; he became Military Assistant when General Joffre was made a Corps Commander, In 1916, he was in the line as a Brigadier-General; in December of that year he became Chief of Staff to Joffre. After the War, he was for six years on a Military Mission in Brazil. In 1925, he was Commander-in-Chief in French Syria, where he suppressed an armed rebellion. In 1935, he was Vice-President of the Conseil Supérieur de la Guerre; in 1938, he became Chief of the General Staff of National Defence.

During the years before the war, some of the best minds of the French Army were pressing for a modern army of tanks, aeroplanes and mechanised cavalry, with an extension of the Maginot Line from Douzy to the sea. Unfortunately, these reforms and improvements were incomplete when the campaign began.

The right of General Georges' Group of Armies lay behind the strong defensive system known as the Maginot Line, which had been completed along the eastern frontiers of France as far as Douzy, nearly five miles south-east from Sedan. From this point to the sea near Dunquerque, the frontier defences were neither complete nor of a permanent nature. There were systems of trenches, with barbed-wire, hidden machine-gun posts and covered battery positions, several ancient fortresses, and various natural obstacles, such as rivers and the great canal systems fed by them. In general, the civil world, ignorant and careless of military matters, supposed that the Maginot Line had been completed to the sea, and that France lay safe behind an impregnable rampart. This illusion, though very widely spread by newspaper articles all over the world, was not shared by soldiers.

The Maginot Line was indeed a great fortress, cunningly devised to withstand any attack of the kinds known in the last war except the attack which had most nearly succeeded. It stopped short at the point where the frontier turns to the west of north. From that point France had little protection from any repetition of the attack through the Luxembourg and Belgium, which in 1914 had come so close to Paris and victory.

The defenders of northern France were these: On the left lay the sea. In French practice, a coast is commanded by the Admiral of the sector. Dunquerque, its surroundings, and the seaward end of the frontier were garrisoned by French soldiers under the command of the Admiral of that part of the coast, known by our troops as "Admiral Nord".

To the right of Admiral Nord's command lay the left of General Georges' group, the Seventh French Army. It stretched from near Dunquerque to near Armentières. It consisted of two corps and an armoured division. To the right of the Seventh French Army the British Expeditionary Force lay. It held a line from near Bailleul to near Laplaigne. It consisted of three corps. To the right of the B.E.F. lay the First French Army from near Laplaigne to near Montbliard. It consisted of three corps.

To the right of the First French Army, mainly behind permanent defences, lay the Ninth French Army, under General André Georges Corap. Much of this army lay behind the Maginot Line proper.

For the first eight months of the war, all this Group of Armies remained quiet. The men passed the winter strengthening their lines, completing training and equipment, and accumulating their stores. They faced a friendly frontier, and though occasionally visited by enemy aeroplanes, such attacks were not serious.

During all the winter, it might be said that our Air Force alone was actively and very dangerously employed. The winter was unusually dry and perhaps the very coldest within living memory. In bitter cold, the dangers of flying are much increased; since ice and snow may overweight the wings, and water, oil and pilots may be frozen. Throughout the winter our Air Force made photographic and other reconnaissances over the greater part of Germany, and through stress of weather lost very heavily. Of air-fighting, there was comparatively little; the war on land had not yet begun in the west.

Even in the south, on the Maginot Line proper, where the garrison faced the enemy, the fighting was never more than patrolling, raiding and bombardment. It was a part of General Gamelin's scheme to reserve all weighty offensive action. He strictly forbade the bombing of military positions in Germany. In all those eight months, troop concentrations, factories, aerodromes, oil-works, railway junctions and sidings within the German frontiers were left unbombed, even when it was known that great movements were preparing and evil being made ready.

In the last war, France lost more than a million of her best young men; her soil and many thousands of her homes were invaded, desecrated and destroyed. For more than four years, a province of France three hundred miles long by from twenty to forty miles broad, was blasted into ruin so completely that in all that expanse scarcely one house was left undamaged or one tree alive. In many places, villages had been so blown to dust that only a redness of the soil from powdered brick showed where the place had been. More than once, during the last war, I saw old Frenchmen standing in these desolations weeping. They had had leave to return to their homes, to dig up valuables which they had hastily buried; there they stood weeping because they were utterly unable to recognise the site; they could not tell where their homes had stood. No doubt, the instinct of the race was to build such a defensive line that the soil and the homes of France should not again be so desecrated and destroyed. In obedience to this instinct, the line was planned, begun and half achieved. In building the line, they showed the world that in their next war they meant to stand on the defensive. Of all the countless heroic deeds of the last war none meant more to them than the defence of Verdun. It has been said by returning soldiers that the defenders of the Maginot Line bore on their uniforms little buttons printed with the phrase once so famous at Verdun: "On ne passera pas", "No one shall get by". As at Verdun they meant to stand on the Line, and keep the enemy from passing. We, as France's ally, with an army under her orders, were committed to her strategical idea. It may be that this feeling for the defensive, no doubt a racial prompting or instinct, came partly from exhaustion. In the Great War, the French had put into four terrible years the effort of a century. A million of their strongest had been killed; all who had returned from the front had been tested beyond their strength; all the young men of the war-time classes had been born in conditions of anxiety and nervous strain. Throughout France, as in all the other lands which had had great losses, there was a subtle exhaustion due to the four years of over-effort.

No doubt, there was deep exhaustion also throughout Germany; but after some years of exhaustion and despair, this was shaken from the mind by thirst for revenge. This thirst was made intense by craft and excited by hope. For six years, the nation thirsted, maddened and was hateful, while it gave to its preparation for vengeance all the fury and energy of savage religion. The results were like those seen when revolutionary France attacked Europe and struck down nation after nation.

DURING the months of war, Holland and Belgium had lived in dread of invasion by the Germans. They had endeavoured to placate their neighbour by the keeping of the strictest neutrality, by enduring patiently insult after insult and the violation of their territory by German aeroplanes. They lived under continual threat. They saw their enemy massed along their frontiers; they knew that his traitors were at work within their cities, and his spies everywhere preparing their destruction. From time to time, as in November and in mid-April, both countries felt that the invasion would begin within a few hours. Both alarms were met by gathering of troops and preparation for flooding. On both occasions the storm threatened but did not break. Many people here thought that it would never break, since both lands could supply Germany with useful goods, and both made sure guards to the German metal-working area near Essen and Dusseldorf. While Holland and Belgium remained independent states they were not trespassed over by any Allied aeroplane, save on two or three occasions, by accident, stress of weather and in fog.

Both the Netherlands and Belgium had received solemn assurances from the enemy that their integrity would be respected if they preserved a strict neutrality. Their behaviour was of the strictest correctness. In the years of the threat of war which preceded 1st September, 1939, both countries showed their strict neutrality by refusing to discuss the possibility of a combination which might at the least lessen the certainty of war, or at the best, make resistance possible if war came. They refused to permit what are called "staff talks" between their own general staffs and those of the Allies.

When the enemy invaded Poland and helped to bring about her ruin, the Allied ambassadors in both countries again asked that such staff talks might be held. In both countries the requests were refused. Both countries from time to time received friendly assurances from Germany. In the Reichstag, on 30th January, 1937, Herr Hitler said: "The German Government has assured Belgium and Holland of its readiness to recognise these States at any time as inviolable neutral territories and to guarantee them."

As there was some doubt in Holland as to what assurances had been meant, enquiries were made in Berlin. After these had been made the Netherlands Government "informed the German

Government that they, with every appreciation of the good intentions manifested in the offer, would not be prepared to conclude with any country a treaty concerning the inviolability of their territory. Such inviolability was for them axiomatic and therefore could not form the subject of any treaty which they might conclude".

In the Reichstag, on 28th April, 1939, Herr Hitler said: "I was pleased that a number of European States availed themselves of these declarations by the German Government to express and emphasise their desire, too, for absolute neutrality. This applies to Holland, Belgium, Switzerland, Denmark, etc. I have never written a single line or made a single speech displaying a different attitude towards the above-mentioned States".

On the 26th of August, 1939, the German Minister at The Hague conveyed to the Netherlands Minister for Foreign Affairs "an assurance from his Government that they would respect in every particular the neutrality of the Netherlands. In return they expected that the Netherlands Government would take all steps to maintain and defend it themselves".

In the Reichstag on the 6th October, 1939, Herr Hitler said: "The new Reich has endeavoured to continue the traditional German friendship with Holland. It has neither found any existing differences with that State nor created any new ones. As soon as I took over the Government, I tried immediately to create friendly relations with Belgium. I renounced any revision and any wish for revision. The Reich has raised no demands likely to be considered a threat to Belgium".

By a declaration of 13th October, 1937, the Government of the Reich solemnly confirmed its determination to make no attempt on the sacredness and integrity of Belgium in any circumstance, and to respect always Belgian territory unless, of course, Belgium should help any military action against Germany in a war in which Germany might be engaged. The Government of the Reich also said that it was ready to give help in Belgium in case she should be the object of attack or invasion. On the 26th August, 1939, in a *démarche spontanée,* the German Government solemnly renewed the engagement of the 13th October, 1937.

Though neither country gave to the enemy any least shadow of cause for complaint and though both gave many great advantages, they were none the better treated. In the first eight months of the war, Belgium lost by German action, not less than a dozen ships sunk and twenty-nine men drowned. Holland lost by German action, not less than twenty-five ships sunk and 175 men drowned.

During the war, Germany requested Holland to watch over her interests in South Africa and in the Cameroons. To some, this seemed "an excellent sign of Germany's intention to leave Holland out of the war".

It may now be well to consider the preparations made by Germany for preserving the sacredness and integrity of Belgium, and for repaying her obligations to Holland.

CERTAIN imaginative men, considering what the next war would be like, decided that henceforth "the defensive", as it was practised in trenches in the Great War, would put a strain on men such as no nation would long endure. These theorists, or cranks, as men of imagination are called, conceived that the abundant and powerful use of aeroplanes and tanks might break up even the strongest defensive system in a few hours. Our imaginative men, and those of France, propounded these theories in books, which in Germany were read and acted upon.

Germany, seeing, in the last war, what should be avoided at all costs, created a vast air force and a mechanical army, such as the world had not yet seen. With the partner in her crime, she waged a war in Spain to test her imagined tactics. In Poland, she tried the combination upon a large scale. After the destruction of Poland, she quietly prepared to let loose upon her friendly neighbours her tested and improved new army.

The new and powerful thing in this army is the armoured division. The Germans call this formation the Panzer Division (Panzer means armour-plate, breast-plate, or cuirass). As much has been said and written about these things, and as their results are now widely displayed in the ruins of civilised Europe, this description of them may be given. They were the chief cause of the ruin which befell the Allies in this campaign; the following is the kind of thing they were, as far as is at present known.

Each German armoured division consists of the following:

1. A reconnaissance unit equipped with light, medium and heavy armoured cars, with wireless installations, machine-guns and machine-pistols. With this unit are the engineer shock troops. These are men picked from the division and trained in certain tasks of demolition which may clear the way for the tanks. These engineers are always well forward, sometimes on motor-cycles and usually in small detachments. There is about one company of them in each division.

2. A tank brigade, of two tank regiments, each containing about 200 tanks. The brigade contains light, medium and heavy tanks of from 6 to about 36 tons. Rumours have been spread of big tanks of 70 and even of 90 tons, but rumour in war is seldom true. The

48

average tank was something over thirty tons, with a mean radius of action of just under 100 miles, and burning, when under way, about thirty gallons of petrol an hour. The fuel-tank holds about 150 gallons; some later types are said to have second fuel-tanks. Some bigger types are said to use heavy oil, not petrol, for fuel and to go 300 miles without replenishing. Most of the tanks used in the campaign bore tough, light, steel shields over their fronts, as the Polish campaign had shown that they needed extra protection. It is said that every tank is followed by a second crew somewhere in the following lorries.

3.   An infantry brigade consisting of one regiment carried in lorries and one motor-cycle battalion.

4.   A unit of anti-tank guns.

5.   A regiment of motor artillery containing two field batteries, each of three troops of four 10.5 cm. (4.14-inch) gun-howitzers. (Twenty-four field-guns to the regiment).

In some divisions a medium battery of four 10.5 cm. guns and eight 5.9-inch howitzers seem to have been added from Corps artillery.

6.   An engineer battalion, with pioneers and pontoonists.

7.   A signal battalion with telephones, radio, etc.

8.   Medical and supply units, with repair train competent to fit new tracks to tanks, and supplies of ammunition, petrol, oils, greases and spares. It was thought that some of the repair train travelled in light tanks fitted out to carry spares and tools.

All these units move by machine of some sort. A full division might need perhaps 1,500 vehicles. In addition, the division has the services of—

9.   An air force squadron for reconnaissance. Every armoured division carried with it at intervals a very full equipment of anti-aircraft guns, light and heavy, with searchlights of unusual power; these travel with the advancing force. In addition, a plentiful supply of all these weapons is left at important points along the line of the advance, at road junctions and bridges.

By this precaution, they deny to their enemies the benefit of swift and sure reconnaissance and give to themselves comparative safety of supply.

There were said to be ten or twelve of these Panzer Divisions employed against the Allies; two to the north of the Albert Canal, two between Maastricht and Givet; the rest in the gap between Givet and Sedan.

The air force which had been built up to work with these divisions was the biggest in the world. The tactics devised for their joint attack were as follows.

The attack begins with a widely-spread bombing of the enemy's back areas, railways, bridges, dumps, headquarters, and especially his aerodromes. In the last war, an attack began with a heavy artillery barrage, sometimes lasting at a frightful intensity for a week on end, with an expense of many thousands of tons of shells, the wearing out of many cannon, and the complete exhaustion of whole armies. The armoured division uses instead of this barrage a series of dive-bombing attacks upon the lines of the opposing troops. The bombers are in great force. They come down from four thousand to within one thousand feet at four hundred miles an hour, sometimes as many as three or four hundred bombers at a time in groups of three, and drop, each, five bombs in a salvo. In some cases the salvo may contain a ton of high explosive. In many cases the bombs have been so made as to give a shrill screaming whistle as they fall. Those who have heard them say that this whistle is not nearly so alarming as the roar of the engines sweeping down.

This dive-bombing is much less fatal than bombardment; it is said not to cause very heavy casualties; but troops cannot be moved while it goes on, for if they do they are at once machine-gunned. It has a demoralising effect on all who endure it; and the effect is, of course, strongest where discipline is weakest.

While the back areas and lines are thus bombed, the engineer shock troops dash out to clear any obstacles which may impede the advance of the tanks. Their advance is often covered by smoke or by heavy supporting fire. They try to blast away the obstacles by devices known as Bangalore torpedoes (sliding planks, studded with grenades, which are thrust below the obstacle and exploded by fuse) and pole-charges (grenades or explosives tied to the end of a pole, thrust under the obstacle and then fired).

When the bombing of the lines has cowed the troops and checked the batteries of the enemy, the tanks advance.

The aim of the Panzer attack is to probe for the weak place and push into it in force the instant it is found or made, to drive through it as fast as possible on as many roads as possible, to broaden the point as much as possible, to seize positions as far distant as possible, to send back wireless reports of what they find, to call up bombers if they meet trouble, and to hold on, in their moving forts, till the infantry can come up in lorries in support. Speed and surprise are ever good weapons in war; they are of the essence of Panzer Division attack. Perhaps one-third of their total effect is the alarm given by their appearance far behind the supposed battle-line; the knowledge that even one or two have got through is enough to make soldiers uneasy and citizens scared. Something of the same effect of alarm and disquiet behind the lines had been won in France in the war of 1870 by the active use everywhere of small cavalry patrols.

This disquiet becomes greater the farther from the line they can appear; they are therefore thrust forward with no regard for anything save speed. The advance is pressed; there is behind it always a sufficient weight of bomber force to clear what opposition may be improvised. Even on bad roads the tanks can move much faster than troops can march. In France, the German bombers made it difficult for troops to use the railway.

Troops having an advantage can always make efforts which seem surprising. The effect aimed at by the Panzer Divisions was swift success. They were ordered to push on, regardless. They seem not to have bothered much about supply, but to have lived on what they could find. For petrol they depended on what their aeroplanes could bring them to particular points. No doubt they found a good deal of fuel and of lubricant in the towns they surprised as they advanced. The rush of their raid brought them success. The method of their army was swiftly established behind them. It is said that within a week they had a pipe-line for fuel running from Germany. What is said in war is not always true.

To help them in their task the enemy high command used cunning means of spreading distrust and terror among the peoples attacked. They placed agents at many points in the threatened country long before the war. Their diplomatists and consuls fermented and spread unrest; they also enlisted and trained traitors for particular services.

In Holland, their diplomatists started to drive an underground passage from the German Embassy towards the Dutch War Office. This was only stopped by some exceptionally tough concrete foundations across their path. Their Military Attaché, on the plea of going to see the bulbs, visited the posts of Dutch soldiers near Rotterdam and sent full particulars of their dispositions to his friends across the border a few hours before the attack began.

The destruction of Holland was prepared by much treachery and cunning. Before the invasion, Dutch uniforms and costumes were smuggled into Germany and copied. When the invasion began, many German agents appeared dressed in Dutch costume or uniform, sometimes as market women, civilians, postmen, car conductors, street-cleaners, priests, seamen or soldiers, and suddenly shot down Dutch officers, policemen and troops. Almost immediately great numbers of parachutists were dropped from aeroplanes in a wide circle round the seat of government at The Hague. These first parachutists were nearly all young desperadoes who had been told that they might shoot at anybody and take for theirs whatever they happened to find. Some of them were as young as sixteen, and few were more than twenty. They shot at anybody who came by, with machine-guns and pistols, they sent important information back by portable wireless sets, and occupied a great many troops before they were finally rounded up. It is thought that Holland received first and last about 15,000 of these, of whom about 13,000 were killed. The later parachutists were less dangerous than the first batches.

The first effort of the Germans in Holland was to seize the aerodromes. They had so great a strength in the air that they were able to destroy the Dutch fighter squadrons and succeed in this. As soon as they had seized the aerodromes, large numbers of soldiers were brought up in troop-carrying aeroplanes. After this, bombing, murder, and overwhelming weight of attack soon put the country out of action.

The campaign had been planned with the utmost possible care; just before the invasion began, great numbers of magnetic mines were dropped in the mouths of all rivers and harbours throughout the country. Low-flying aeroplanes came over the towns and fired machine-guns at the citizens. A group of about 100 Germans disguised as Dutch soldiers marched behind a Dutch battalion and suddenly opened fire on the soldiers from behind. Many Germans advanced behind parties of women and children whom they compelled to march in front of them. Wherever German troops appeared, they had with them guides who had been employed in

Holland as domestic servants or in business. Each group dropped from the parachutes carried two days' rations. Each had a special purpose. They knew the houses they were to seize and the people they were to shoot. Those of them who wore Dutch uniforms had code words and signs by which their friends could tell them at a glance from the Dutch. One useful and simple sign was the corner of a handkerchief pinned outside an outer pocket by two pen- or pencil-clips. All the Germans in Holland had identity-cards. It is thought that all of them knew what was about to happen and took some part in the attack or in preparation for its success. Both in Holland and Belgium some of the first points seized were bridges. The parachutists wearing Dutch or Belgian uniforms, and speaking good Dutch, French or Walloon, stopped and seized civilian cars and proceeded in them to seize the bridges.

Twelve parachutists can be dropped from a Junker 52 aeroplane, in from 6-10 seconds, from a height of 300 feet. The times for their arrival were usually shortly before or after daybreak. Most of their gear was dropped separately in containers, also by parachute. The gear was of many sorts, small mortars, automatic guns, hand-grenades, flame-throwers, motor-cycles, bicycles, and even motor-cycle side-cars fitted with machine-guns. Sometimes para-chutists appeared to surrender and would have a bomb ready in each hand for those who believed. Some of them were dressed as Dutch schoolboys or school-girls. A good many who were to act as guides were real girls dressed as nurses of the hospitals near which they landed. Servant-girls who were to serve as guides were landed in places where they had previously worked as domestic servants. Those dressed as girls, both men and women, carried baskets full of hand-grenades made to look like provisions or vegetables. They had automatic guns hidden under their clothes and some carried poisonous cigarettes and chocolate. Among them were some strange people who had no idea what they were to do, except to shoot at anything they saw. These were perhaps drugged or mad. Certain aircraft dropped poisoned cigarettes and chocolates on exhausted Dutch troops. Most of the parachutists were completely un-scrupulous. One man on being rescued by a Dutch soldier from drowning shot his rescuer on landing. Most of them appeared dizzy and dazed on reaching; the ground. It always took a parachute party some few minutes to make ready after landing. Both in Holland and

Belgium signs in chalk and paint for the guidance of the German troops appeared instantaneously on telegraph poles and buildings. Undoubtedly the first success of these parachutists was considerable, especially in Holland, where in the disguise of Dutch officers, they shot so many soldiers that solitary officers were often shot on sight lest they should prove to be Germans.

In Belgium, there seems to be no doubt that parachutists were dropped all over the country, disguised as French, Belgian or British officers, as priests, nuns, doctors, civilians and women. But throughout Belgium there were very many secret agents already placed for action and well trained in what they had to do. The aim in Holland was to paralyse. That was not neglected in Belgium, where much was undoubtedly done to stir up the bitter feeling between Fleming and Walloon, but the chief aim in Belgium was to spread terror and block the roads with refugees. From the very first, much craft was shown in the prevention of accurate information. In the night of the 9th–10th May their agents cut countless wires in Belgium and Northern France. It was said that these agents had flexible wires which could be tossed over the telegraph wires by the road and when pulled cut them through. So many wires were cut in the Luxembourg that the news of the German advance never reached the line of the Meuse. With this prevention of information came much craft in the spreading of false reports. Before dawn of the 10th, all the important cities in Belgium had been bombed. By daylight on that day countless German agents, men and women, were busy persuading the inhabitants to escape while there was still time. They said that it was necessary to start at once since the enemy was only two miles away. Everyone of middle age in Belgium remembered the last German invasion, the thousands of murders, the ruthless robberies, and the brutal deportations when multitudes of young men and women had been taken into Germany to work as slaves. When the people had been terrified by the bombing, they listened only too readily to these spreaders of panic. At this first moment, there was a want of direction in Belgium. No decisive word was spoken to stop this blocking of the roads. Private cars, the sale of petrol, and the use of the roads, were not forbidden. Anybody could still go anywhere. At once, throughout Belgium, this rush to some imagined safety began. Men and women loaded up their carts, lorries, ox-carts, horse-carts and perambulators, They drove out their horses, their herds of cattle and what was much worse, their flocks of sheep, and began the unhappy march. Those who were in the north went south, those who were in the east went west. Presently the two streams ran into each other and merged. Presently the merged stream came up against the French and English armies trying to get up to help their country. All soldiers agreed that this crowding of the roads was one of the main causes of our trouble.

It was all a part of the enemy plan. The enemy argued that these refugees would block the roads to us and that the French and English would look upon these people as their friends, and be patient with them. In this they were right. Our armies were very patient with them, and on every road they delayed our advance. But this was but a small part of the trouble. Among those multitudes, and it must be remembered that there were some millions of them, were countless skilled spies carrying small wireless transmitters by which they at once reported what troops were coming by particular roads.

These spies were everywhere. They spread false rumours of disasters. To the English they said that the French had been defeated, and to the French that England had been destroyed. All telegraph and telephone wires near the road were cut, and when re-layed were cut again within half an hour, and sometimes burned out in stretches of fifty yards. Forged notices appeared on buildings. Frequent false orders and false directions were given to troops. At many points throughout the campaign enemy agents fired at our troops and at the refugees from houses. More than one case is reported of enemy agents driving along the roads in cars, shooting at people near the cross-roads and then turning out of the stream of traffic and getting away.

In the Belgian cities the aeroplanes frequently dropped what seemed to be pencils. If children or others picked up these seeming pencils they exploded in their hands. At night they dropped in the cities noisy crackers which banged for a minute or two, to make the citizens think that people were fighting in the streets. Parachutists were sometimes seen descending. Men running to intercept them often found that the figure was a dummy, which exploded when touched. It was thought that in the bigger towns enemy agents contrived to set going the airraid signals every ten minutes both by day and night. This continual melancholy wailing had a shocking effect on people's nerves. But there were air-raids almost every ten minutes. Throughout Belgium aeroplanes were diving down upon the roads at intervals, dropping bombs on the traffic and machine-gunning the people. Some of the bombs had delayed-action fuses and exploded long after they had fallen. Wherever the poor people turned, they saw the smoke of burning towns and homes, heard the roar of bombers, and the crash of bombs, and often the rattle of machine-guns just over their heads. As they went along some of them piled mattresses above their carts to keep out bullets, and green boughs to hide them from the bombers. Many of them were old, infirm people. Very many of them were women and children. Of all the sad sights of the campaign those unfortunates were the saddest. How many thousands of them were murdered by the enemy, or died of exposure, misery, want and heart-break, will never be known.

It was said and believed that certain widely spread advertisements of chicory were helps to the enemy. Each advertisement peeled easily off its board and bore upon its back a map of the district in which it was.

Enemy agents repeatedly discovered where headquarters were, and then cut, in the crops or in the ground, rude arrows pointing towards the house so that aeroplanes could tell at a glance where the headquarters lay. They then bombed the house at leisure. These arrows were often made conspicuous by gramophone records or metal discs. Two cases are reported of the enemy's attacking troops being disguised as women. "In black clothes with yellow sashes." Men were sometimes found registered as day labourers yet carrying suspicious quantities of Belgian money. Large numbers of Belgian uniforms were sometimes found laid out in lonely houses ready for enemy agents coming with the refugees. There were frequent cases of men in the stream of refugees shooting at soldiers and at sentries. In some parts of Belgium, certainly, the inhabitants led the enemy against our patrols. On the 28th May, one post was taken from the rear by a party of Germans in civilian clothing and armed with Tommy guns.

On the 21st, a party of British troops was attacked by seventy-five soldiers disguised as civilians. On that same day two Germans speaking English and dressed in British uniforms were caught ordering the inhabitants to take to the roads.

One of the painful things of the campaign may be briefly noticed. Over an immense area the horses, cattle, pigs, sheep, rabbits and poultry were abandoned on the farms without food or water. Our soldiers did what they could always to give them access to food and water. Cows were milked when possible. Orders were given that abandoned dogs should be killed. Many were killed, but hundreds followed the B.E.F. right across Belgium to Dunquerque.

In the foregoing, instances have been given of what happened during the campaign. Let us now turn to the days before the beginning of the trouble, when the event lay upon the knees of the gods and the bombs had not begun to fall.

It is an interesting fact that a few weeks before the blow fell, some suggestions made in this country "that acts of treachery were impending in Holland" were denied by the Dutch authorities.

As enemy agents were setting abroad the rumour that Switzerland was to be the next victim, it seemed likely that Holland and Belgium were doomed.

On Sunday, the 5th May, the weather experts at the enemy headquarters must have seen from the reports that the prospects of settled fair weather were good. By the next day they had improved.

By Tuesday, the 7th, they had improved still more. At this time, it must be remembered, the enemy weather experts had the advantage of the weather reports from Holland and Belgium, based on observations from their ships in the Atlantic. They knew from these that a great anticyclone was slowly edging eastward from the Atlantic, bringing the almost certainty of dry weather for the movement of tanks and troops, and of clear skies for attacking aeroplanes.

In the afternoon of 7th May, a minister at The Hague telephoned that the Dutch had cancelled all leave for the defence forces, the munitions workers and soldiers with the active army. "This," he said, "is a precautionary measure having regard to the international situation." Obstructions were placed on roads and on the landing-grounds of aerodromes. Mines were laid under roads and bridges; all the frontier posts were ordered to be specially watchful.

On the 9th, all the prospects seemed good for settled fair weather; indeed, it seemed certain that the fine weather would last. German military attachés at The Hague told the Dutch Ministers that the Berlin authorities could not understand why the Dutch were taking so many precautions.

At a little before 4 on the morning of the 10th, without offence given, without provocation. of any kind, without declaration of war, the enemy descended upon, Holland with bombs, parachutists and troop-carrying aeroplanes.

On Belgium and the Luxembourg he fell with all these things, backed up by tanks and swiftly moving mechanical columns.

The German Minister to Holland delivered a message that all resistance was useless and that if the country did resist, both the country and its political existence would be annihilated.

The German ambassador in Brussels read to the Belgian Minister for Foreign Affairs a long document to the following effect.

"The German Government, being convinced of the impending entry of French and British troops into Belgium, has decided to come to Belgium's aid with forces which are of such a nature as will brook no resistance. If Belgium behaves, Germany will guarantee her present territory, her colonies, dynasty, etc. If, on the other hand, she resists, she will be overwhelmed".

No other declaration of war was made by the Germans. The paper read by the German Ambassador in Brussels was published and broadcast in Germany as an Order of the Day. This Order, in the translations which I have seen, states that "the Germans enter Belgium and Holland because the English and French are attempting, by employment of a gigantic manœuvre of distraction in South-East Europe, to thrust forward into the Ruhr district over Holland and Belgium."

The atrocities which followed this morning's crime are now a matter of sorrowful history.

1. The Secretary of State for War, Anthony Eden (centre), leaving the War Office with Lord Gort (right), Commander in Chief of the British Expeditionary Force during the Flanders campaign and Sir John Dill, commanding officer of I Corps in September 1939, who became Chief of the Imperial General Staff on 27th May 1940 at the height of the Dunkirk evacuation.

2. The downtrodden and dispossessed. The plight of the refugees, such as these families in Belgium, was close to the heart of John Masefield.

3. The calm before the storm. British troops, well dug in on the Franco-Belgian border, take a meal break during the period known as the 'phoney war'.

4. Men of the Gloucestershire Regiment man a hastily improvised anti-tank post on the outskirts of the town of Cassel, one of the key defensive block points on the western wall of the B.E.F.'s escape corridor to Dunkirk.

5. British soldiers advancing to new positions pass weary refugees fleeing the war zone.

6. On the move. A convoy of British soldiers raise a smile for the camera as they motor along the lanes of Flanders.

7. Patience. Hundreds of men make a human snake across the sands as they queue in orderly fashion whilst waiting their turn for evacuation from the beaches east of Dunkirk.

8. On the beach. Port installations burn ferociously in the distance as allied troops mill around awaiting orders.

9. Bray Dunes east of Dunkirk. Men wade out to small boats in a scene that characterises the lack of organisation during the early days of the evacuation.

10. Life in the dunes. At certain locations groups of leaderless men congregate amongst the sand dunes waiting for someone to tell them what to do.

11. Mind the gap. Troops using scaling ladders and planks in a hazardous transfer to H.M.S. *Harvester*, berthed at the eastern Mole of Dunkirk harbour.

12. Utter exhaustion. For those men still awake, the sheer relief at being rescued is etched into their faces.

13. Packed like sardines. An overloaded ship enters Dover harbour with its precious cargo of rescued British soldiers.

14. Home at last. The B.E.F. lost almost all its guns, vehicles and heavy equipment during the 1940 Flanders Campaign whilst many men lost items of uniform and personal weapons in the helter-skelter retreat to Dunkirk.

15. The Dunkirk spirit takes root. Not yet off the ship, these returning British soldiers nevertheless manage to put on a cheerful show for the cameramen waiting on the Dover quaysides.

16. John Masefield (left) pictured with W.B. Yeats in Dublin in 1935, five years after he became Poet Laureate and five years prior to writing *The Twenty-Five Days*.

The First Day, Friday, 10th May.

"The Belgians first knew that the Germans were attacking when bombs began falling early this morning."

Sixteen civilians were killed and twenty wounded in Brussels alone. One house within thirty yards of the United States Embassy was gutted. Probably every important city in Belgium was bombed just before daylight on this day. Belgium's most important aerodrome called The Secret Aerodrome at St. Trond was very heavily bombed. At the same time the airraid warnings sounded all over the lines of the B.E.F. in France. Enemy bombers came over our headquarters near Arras; waves of them passed to attack Doullens and our aerodromes at Abbeville, Boulogne, Le Touquet, Calais and elsewhere. Possibly some of these raiding planes dropped men here and there to cut telegraph and telephone wires between the Canche, the Authie and the Somme; certainly enemy sympathisers cut them. At the same time the machines, the treasons and surprises long since made ready were set going. In a Memorandum handed to the victims that morning, the Germans declared that they were "coming to safeguard the neutrality of these two countries by all the military means at the disposal of the Reich". The Memorandum added that "the German troops did not come as enemies to the Belgian and Dutch peoples".

Early that morning, the Belgian and Netherlands representatives in London appealed to His Majesty's Government, stating:

1. That German troops had invaded their territories in defiance of solemn undertakings;
2. That their Governments had decided to resist this aggression; and that they appealed to the Governments of France and the United Kingdom for help, feeling sure that, as in the past, our efforts joined with their own would achieve the triumph of right.

In reply, H.M. Government assured the Netherlands and the Belgian Ambassadors that we should stand firmly by the side of the Dutch and Belgian peoples in the struggle so wantonly forced upon them. A similar assurance was sent to H.R.H. the Grand Duchess of Luxembourg.

One hour after the Belgian appeal for help had been received in London, the Royal Air Force received signals permitting them to fly over the three invaded countries of Holland, Belgium and Luxembourg. Within the next two hours our photographic and strategical reconnaissances were away to the north and the east to see what could be seen. It was fine summer weather, tending to be hazy in the east, beyond the enemy frontier. Great numbers of photographs were taken. While these sorties were getting under way, the French High Command issued orders to the B.E.F. to prepare to move at once to the support of the Belgian and Dutch Armies.

The neutrality of the two nations had made it impossible for us to work out with them in detail any plan to resist an invasion of the kind now in progress, but the Conseil Supérieur de la Guerre had worked out with the B.E.F. a scheme for advancing into Belgium if she were attacked. This scheme, known to the French as B/H (Belgique/Hollande) and to the English as Plan D, or the Dyle Plan, was now ordered and put into action. At once, along the northern frontier of France, the armies moved forward. "On partait," as M. Lauzanne wrote a few weeks later, "Pour sauver une maison dont on avait été rigoureusement tenu à l'écart et dont on ignorait jusqu'a l'aménagement."

Some of the difficulties may be mentioned. It is never easy for the armies of three or four nations to work in close accord together in difficult operations. The joins and overlappings of such armies are always points of weakness. The ignorance of the different services of each other, the subtle and profound differences of national temper, tongue and prejudice, tax any tact and strain every sympathy. These ignorances and differences make it easy for spies and enemy agents to work everywhere in and behind the lines of such composite armies. The difficulties of coordinating movements are enormous; the jealousies of commands often intense, and the different systems, supplies, ways, calibres and armaments endless causes of confusion. However, two valorous and friendly nations, one of them a brave ally in the last war, had cried to us for help, and neither the French nor our own men hesitated for an instant. Help so asked must be given.

60

The Dyle Plan was designed to move the armies along the French northern frontier north and northeastward till they covered, or helped to cover, all the Belgian northern and eastern frontiers. On the left, the Seventh French Army was to enter Walcheren and North Beveland, to occupy a line Turnhout-Breda in Holland, to guard the great islands in the Escaut Estuary, and to support the Dutch on that flank. They were to move roughly to a line twenty-five miles north-east of Antwerp. When there, they would have on their right the bulk of the Belgian Army, which was on the line Malines-Antwerp. The B.E.F. was to march forward to the right of the main Belgian Army and take up a position near Louvain along the little River Dyle. On the right of the B.E.F. the First French Army would extend the line in front of Gembloux and Charleroi to the Foret de Trélon, where its right would touch the left of the Ninth French Army.

This great movement forward of some 450,000 men began at once, according to the order. The three enormous hordes advanced, with their multitudes of cars, lorries, guns and services, their signals, supplies and hospitals. The Seventh Army had to go about a hundred miles; the B.E.F. about seventy miles; the First Army about fifty miles. As they crossed the frontier into Belgium, the men of the B.E.F. were received with enthusiasm by the Belgians, who well remembered their comrades in the last war. Our soldiers were given flowers, refreshments and applause; the guns and tanks were hung with lilac.

The air reports soon came in from the reconnaissance flights; fires were burning in Antwerp and Brussels; Belgian and Dutch troops were moving to position, and great columns of enemy were on the roads leading to the frontiers. Attacks were being made at different points along the Belgian eastern frontier. These air reports were obtained with difficulty and danger; the enemy had a great strength in the air; he was bombing all aerodromes and many other places, towns, villages and all places likely to contain troops. "He had clouds of bombers, backed up by fighters." What machines we had were used all day long; as fast as they could be refuelled and given fresh ammunilion, they took off again and again. The average time flown that day was seven hours per pilot; some of the pilots went out seven times. They brought down forty-nine enemy machines of all kinds, including one bomber which crashed with a full load of bombs near Hazebrouck and caused many civilian casualties; we lost, in that day, three machines, had one pilot wounded and one other reported missing, who returned unhurt next day. Two more squadrons of our R.A.F. flew to France from England during that day; on arrival, they went out to learn the country; they saw the enormous volume of the enemy air force at work on its bombing of Belgium; they attacked it, when they saw it, and shot down four enemy machines without loss to themselves.

The advance of the B.E.F. was led by the Twelfth Lancers, an admirable force of "mechanised cavalry" under Lieut.-Col. Herbert Lumsden, D.S.O., M.C., who were on the River Dyle and patrolling beyond it before eleven that night. Though the enemy was bombing many places in Belgium, the advance of the Allied armies was not much bombed. Knowing the strength of the enemy air force, some soldiers, who noticed this want of interference, wondered if it were a part of the enemy plan to let us advance unmolested.

The enemy counted on surprise and speed in seizing advantage. The Belgians and their Allies counted upon certain frontier defences and the delays which these might give to the enemy's advance.

The main northern defence of Belgium was the strong, wide, deep ditch of the Albert Canal; in the walls of which were sunken forts and gun positions three to the mile. North of this was a lesser line, the Meuse-Escaut Canal, but this was an outer, lighter line not to be seriously held. On the east, they had the strong line of the gorge of the Meuse, nowhere easy to cross, and defended by very powerful modern forts round the two cities Liege and Namur. Away to the east of the Meuse lies the difficult, wooded country of the Ardennes.

Unfortunately, the north-eastern frontier of Belgium marches with a narrow Dutch province less than twenty miles broad. The capital of this province is Maastricht, which on the 10th of May had three bridges over the Meuse. Most of the security of Belgium depended on these bridges being kept from the enemy's power.

Farther south, the Belgians planned to check the approach of the enemy to the Meuse by blocking the roads and by fighting delaying actions. The Belgian Ardennes were defended by the crack patrols of the Belgian Chasseurs. These troops had orders to hold or delay the enemy advance by rifle- and machine-gun fire; they were to move from point to point by bicycle, checking the enemy where they could; they were to block the roads behind them by felling trees across them. Both in the Ardennes and elsewhere in Belgium, use was to be made of what was called the de Cointet obstacle, a wheeled barrier made of wood and iron in length of four or six yards and much strung about with barbed wire.

These delaying methods were not successful. The Chasseurs were outnumbered, outgunned and out-speeded by the enemy's light tanks and motor-bicycles. They did not delay the advance through the Ardennes, but were driven back before they had felled trees across the roads and made the defiles impassable. The obstacles were speedily blown or dragged out of the way. Moreover, enemy agents dressed as Belgian officers appeared at many places, with orders for the Chasseurs to fall back. These men or other agents cut all telegraph and telephone wires. Meanwhile, in all the frontier districts, agents were telling the inhabitants that the Germans were already only two miles away and that they would infallibly enslave the young, as in the last war. There then began that unhappy rush to some imagined safety which was to continue for the rest of the campaign. Men and women took their children, their chief treasures and their cattle on to roads already thronged with troops and transport moving to defend them.

In the Grand Duchy of Luxembourg, the Customs Officers tried to resist the Germans; some of them were killed, the rest thrust aside. A great strength of the enemy army set forth across the Luxembourg without opposition; news of its coming did not precede it; the wires were down and the scouting planes in front of it too many. Already the great numbers of anti-aircraft guns with the enemy forward units made it hard for reconnaissance flights to bring abundant accurate information back. It has been said that between Maastricht and Mezieres the frontiers were attacked at eleven places. At each place sufficient force was ready to snatch any advantage which might be found.

For the Allies, this 10th of May, was mainly passed upon the roads, moving to the north-east through applauding, welcoming Belgians. All through the day and in the moonlight and haze of the night the streams of motor transport passed. After sunset the entries to towns and all main turnings were well lit by electric glow-lamps, placed there by Traffic Control posts. So far, only important towns had been bombed. The people in some of the country districts had heard nothing of any war; they were busy in the fields as ever in what seemed like deep peace. By moonlight that night our outposts were at Wavre and beyond, finding the little Dyle River not much of an obstacle, and owing to the dry year only two feet deep. An officer rejoining his battalion after leave in England took a taxi to the front from the landing-stage at Boulogne.

During this day, some ships of the Navy stood close-in to the Belgian coast to guard the left flank of the Seventh French Army as it marched north. Other ships went to Dutch waters with troop-ships and demolition parties. Some soldiers were landed in Dutch ports, and some British subjects taken to safety. Early in the after-noon the machine cavalry of the French began to cross the estuary ferry to Flushing. During the afternoon and evening, in spite of bombing from the air, the Belgians worked with our seamen to clear the port of Antwerp of shipping. This task went on day and night for some days under an ever-growing air attack.

The Second Day, Saturday, 11th May.

This was one of the fatal days of the campaign. In the morning, by methods not certainly clear, the enemy got possession of a bridge across the Meuse at Maastricht. All three of these bridges had been prepared for destruction in case of invasion. When the alarm came, one bridge was blown or partly blown by the officer responsible. The other two, one big, one small, were surprised and seized by the enemy before they could be blown. It is said that a few picked men were brought up silently in a glider, and that these men overpowered the bridge guards before the charges could be fired. It is said that a brave Dutch or Belgian officer, whose nation and name I have not yet been able to learn, went out to one bridge, contrived to enter the explosion chamber, fired the charge, and was blown to pieces with the bridge. Possibly this was the southern bridge. Two bridges were in the enemy's possession by 11.15 that morning and were at once made use of by him.

As always, the Germans were very swift to improve their advan-tage; they were ready with the machines, the guns and the men directly the bridges were seized. In waves all day long their dive-bombers came over to shake and destroy the Belgian soldiers defending the crossing. The Belgian Seventh Division was almost destroyed here; the dive-bombers made it impossible for supports to move up. Having seized the bridges, the enemy at once made his bridge-head, by coming across in force, and then thrusting fanwise out, right and left, to make his advance a few miles broad. As always, he had at hand, ready for instant use, the materials for more bridges and a great strength of A.A. guns and searchlights to help him to hold what he had won. By the night of the 11th, he was over the Meuse in sufficient strength to hold his winnings.

At this time our first two Corps were taking up position on the Dyle, some forty-five miles from Maastricht and about 150 miles from the Channel ports, vital to our supply; the French First Army on our right was some fifty or sixty miles from Maastricht. On the western side of Belgium, the French Seventh Army was making a marvellous march into position. Some have thought that this 11th of May decided the campaign against the Belgians. The seizure of the bridge-head at Maastricht had turned and made useless the two main defences of the land, the line of the Meuse and the Albert Canal; the enemy was over both in force. The knowledge that he had done this with weapons against which the Belgians had no defence, for they had no tanks, and had already lost almost all their air force, was disheartening to the whole Belgian Army.

Already, on the second day of the war, they had been forced back everywhere by greater strength than theirs; depression spread swiftly through their army. Their headquarters had had to move back. Some elements in the Army were against the war; there were also divisions in the Belgian nation which might well end her share in the war in a few days. It was said that only King Leopold's influence kept her in the war at all, after this seizing of the Maastricht bridges.

In the afternoon of this second day, the enemy had another great success, he took the small but powerful fort of Eben Emael at the junction of the Meuse and the Albert Canal, four miles south of Maastricht. It is thought that a few very brave, specially picked and trained German soldiers were dropped directly on to the roofs of this fortress, either by parachutes or gliders. These men, when they reached the roofs, at once dropped small bombs and hand-grenades down the ventilating shafts into the fort. These exploded, wrecked the ventilating system, and put much evil-smelling smoke throughout the casemates. Some say that they also put bombs or grenades into the muzzles of the guns. The officers in the forts, when they found what was happening on the roofs, telephoned to neighbouring works to sweep the roofs with fire. This was at once done, and the bombing-party destroyed. However, they had played their part, the mischief had been done; the soldiers inside the fort, being presently overcome by the fumes of explosions and the want of air, surrendered. German gliders are said to carry as many as ten men apiece. Photographs taken after the fall of Eben Emael showed ten gliders inside the defence area.

The enemy told their foreign newspaper correspondents that this success had been won by "a new weapon against which there could be no defence"; the next day, seeing that this tale was succeeding, they called the new weapon "a nerve gas". Many articles about this nerve gas appeared in papers up and down the world. No gas seems to have been used (so far) by the enemy on the western front of this war; but the smoke of some of his grenades is said to smell strongly and to cause a slight sensation of burning in the throat. Soldiers think that these grenades were used at Eben Emael.

All through the late afternoon and evening, our bombers tried to wreck the remaining bridges at Maastricht and to stop the laying of pontoons across the Meuse and the Albert Canal. Word came that all the other bridges had been broken, but that these two were now so strongly guarded by fighter aircraft and guns that no hit could be made upon them.

By the evening of this second day, the enemy had begun his main attack upon the French positions to the south of Givet.

The Third Day, Sunday, 12th May.

The fighting between the 12th and 15th of May decided the campaign. By the morning of the 12th, the Belgian Army was out of heart, the B.E.F. digging-in upon its new positions, the First French Army sending out cavalry patrols toward St. Trond; the Seventh Army away on the left, completing its marvellous march.

To the right of the First French Army the Ninth French Army was moving north-eastward in conformity with the Allied advance. It was said that this army, during the winter, had done less work than any of the armies and that some elements in it lacked discipline.

The movements and positions of the divisions of this army are not now known in England. It became clear that the enemy might come against it in very great strength either on this third day or on the morrow. It was not easy to learn what was coming from Germany. The enemy had enormous strength in the air, and a vast mobile anti-aircraft artillery to keep us from finding out what was advancing. Still, our Air Force was used unsparingly, and brought back disquieting reports. There was a great army pressing south-westward from the Albert Canal and Maastricht, and at least two Panzer divisions coming through the Ardennes. The mechanical cavalry of the First French Army went out to check the enemy coming from Maastricht, and the Royal Air Force undertook to try to delay the enemy at the Meuse and the canal.

The French cavalry met the enemy advance at St. Trond, checked it, and drove it back a little. The Royal Air Force did something to delay the German advance in Holland and made heroic, continued and at last successful forays against the remaining Maastricht bridges. Eight attacks upon these bridges had failed to destroy them. Volunteers for another attempt were called for; all the pilots present came forward; their names written on paper were drawn from a hat, and the crews so chosen went out to try for the ninth time.

The five bombers received orders to wreck the two bridges; three went against the big bridge in advance of the others, two against the smaller. They had with them an escort of three fighters.

About twenty miles from Maastricht, thirty enemy fighters attacked the formation; the three fighters at once attacked the thirty, while the five bombers went on alone in their two groups of three and two. Several of the thirty enemy fighters were shot down.

The bombers went on till they had almost reached the enemy barrage of anti-aircraft fire outside Maastricht. At this point, the two detailed for the smaller bridge were attacked by more enemy fighters, who came on them suddenly from the rear; the bombers swerved and shot down one of these attackers, which "seemed to frighten the others, for they soon sheered off".

A few instants later the two bombers were in the enemy barrage; "the barrage was terrific" and here, as they came down to attack, they had a dreadful experience: "we saw the flight of three bombers, now returning home, caught in the thick of the enemy's fire and all three were lost".

The two came down to 2,000 feet to drop their bombs. "The big bridge looked a sorry mess and was sagging in the middle, hit by the bombs dropped by the three bombers ahead of us". They dropped their own bombs on the lesser bridge. "On looking down we saw that our bridge now matched the other. It sagged in the centre and its iron girders looked far from intact". Turning for home, they found the barrage even more intense than on their coming-in; one bomber was shot down; the other was so badly hit that the pilot gave orders to abandon ship. The rear-gunner jumped first "and we have seen nothing of him since, although we believe he is in a hospital". The pilot (Pilot-Officer Davy) remained in the shattered bomber and brought her safely down at Brussels. Sergeant Mansell, to whose account I am indebted for these vivid details, jumped when the bomber was near Liege and came down by parachute.

Unfortunately, all Belgium was by this time aware of the danger of parachutists. All the populace, as well as all the armies, were looking out for them. A mob of some hundreds gathered to watch the sergeant's descent. When he came down in a garden, he was dragged over the fence. "Men and women held my arms whilst an old and angry man prepared to shoot me. Again I shouted 'Anglais, Anglais,' and I am thankful to say that somebody thought it was just possible that I was telling the truth".

These two were the sole survivors from the attack on the Maastricht bridges. The leaders of the flight of three which destroyed the big bridge, Flying-Officer Donald Garland and Sergeant Thomas Gray, the one aged twenty-two, and the other twenty-six, were awarded posthumous Victoria Crosses.

On this day the Belgian Government decreed that no civilian nor civilian vehicle should use any Belgian road between 10 p.m. and 6 a.m. In the anguish of the time this decree was not regarded nor enforced. They used the roads as never before. Till the end of the campaign, half the population was on the roads, and owners of motor vehicles found it possible to obtain petrol.

The Fourth Day, Monday, 13th May.

On this day, the extreme left was held temporarily at The Hook by a small party of Royal Marines and a Guards battalion. They were attacked from the air and by troops brought up by troop-carrying aeroplanes. They held these attacks, and watched from their position the great blaze and smoke-cloud from the burning oils at Rotterdam, twenty miles to the eastward from them. Away to the south of them, the advanced left of the French Seventh Army in North Beveland and Walcheren was not having much success. The enemy had forestalled them by troops brought up by aeroplane, and by many members of their Fifth Column. National feeling kept the inhabitants of these islands from much sympathy with an invasion of French soldiers, however friendly; the Fifth Column men helped to stir the feeling. The machine-cavalry of the Seventh Army had come so fast and so far that it had outrun its supports and supplies. The troops brought by the enemy aeroplanes were more than enough to hold them. On their right, the Belgians, who had already fought bravely and lost heavily, were falling back, out of heart. Our own troops were engaged at several places on our front between Louvain and Tirlemont; the French, to our right, were also engaged. There came news that the fighting to the south of Givet was becoming more intense.

On this, the day after the never-enforced decree limiting road traffic in Belgium, a multitude of unfortunates reached Merchtem, about twelve miles north-west from Brussels. These were refugees from Holland and from places north of Antwerp, who had already suffered an extreme of misery. Two days before, they had reached Merchtem, trying to go south, and had been ordered back to the north. On their way north the Seventh French Army had barred their passage and sent them south again; now at Merchtem their lot was to be turned north once more.

On this day, near Louvain, there was a gas-alarm, which made some units wear gas-masks. It was presently found that the alarm was due not to a gas-attack but to the blowing fumes from a burning ammonia factory.

The Fifth Day, Tuesday, 14th May.

On the left, the enemy advanced from Rotterdam upon all the Allied positions still held in the south of Holland. For a little while on this day there was talk of trying to embark the Dutch Army, presumably from the Hook of Holland; this was no more than a thing suggested. The main event of the day was the enemy attack upon the French positions near Sedan.

The attack is said to have been preceded by the passing of a wave of aeroplanes making a frightful noise, as of sirens, while diving low.

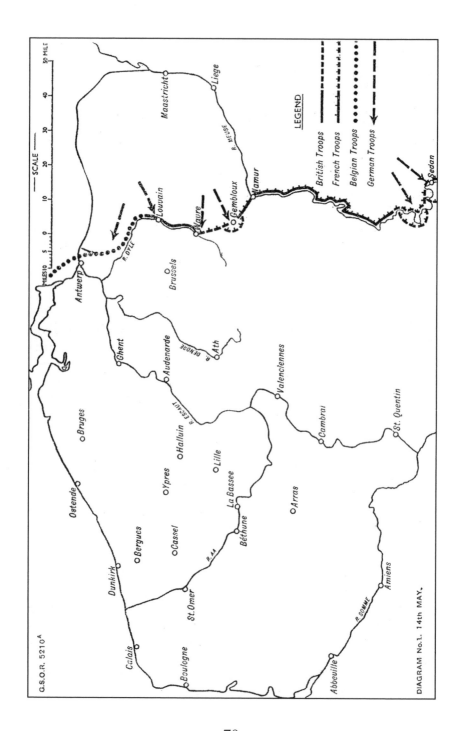

G.S.O.R. 5210ᴬ

DIAGRAM No.1. 14th MAY.

These planes are said to have passed, then returned, and were then followed by others, which fired from machine-guns, and were then followed by the real attack, of dive-bombers with high explosive, screaming bombs, which came almost in a stream, one wave in every ten minutes, all through the day.

The attack came between all that stretch of the Meuse between Mezieres and Sedan. Soldiers who were there have said that the bombing caused comparatively few casualties, but that it had a terrible effect upon the less well-disciplined units.

The attack was skilfully aimed at the point where success would turn both the northern and the eastern lines of French defence. It was a point as vital to France as Maastricht had been to Belgium. Following his practice, the enemy struck it with very great strength: all the roads were busy with streams of enemy for miles to the eastward. The French asked for the help of our Air Force to try to check the advance.

Unfortunately, even a crowded road is difficult to block by bombing. Upset tanks and lorries can be cleared swiftly wherever there are many men. If holes be blown in the road, these can be speedily filled. In the dry weather of that May, the machines could usually turn out of badly-damaged roads to run over the fields. It was found that the enemy was always most adroit at taking cover and very clever at disguising his vehicles against observation from the air.

The help for which the French asked had already been generously given. All the day before, our pilots had been making attacks every two hours on the roads and bridges at Neufchateau and Bouillon, the two great road-junctions to the east of Sedan.

We were without day-bombers, that service in which the enemy was so strong, and by this time, what with losses on the ground and in battle our Air-component Force with the B.E.F. was sadly thinned. Nevertheless, our men went out to help the French near Sedan by bombing bridges, roads and road-junctions, the lines of advancing tanks, cyclists, and lorries, and the ceaseless activity of men making pontoon-bridges or launching rubber-boats. Our men wrecked three permanent and three pontoon-bridges near Sedan; blocked the road near Givonne; fired the woods east of Sedan; damaged Villers bridge; and destroyed the railway-junctions which might serve the enemy in the Luxembourg.

All the traffic on the roads by which the old Emperor's armies had moved in 1870 was bombed and rebombed all day long, in spite of every form of attack from guns and fighters. Weak as our force unhappily was, the men in it were not weak. Sometimes on this day over Sedan they engaged enemy air-forces ten times their strength. One squadron of six fighters attacked a formation of fifty-four counted enemy fighters "and some bombers". Another squadron of six shot down nine enemy planes without loss to themselves.

This resolute, heroic bombing made a great impression on the enemy, and helped the French to counter-attack. It was thought that if this counter-attack had been better supported a very great success might have been won.

The Royal Air Force was to do many self-sacrificing acts of heroism in this campaign: none grander than this. The pilots knew well how desperate the French need was. More than half the aeroplanes used by us were lost in this battle (thirty-five out of sixty-seven); luckily, the crews of five of the lost machines contrived to rejoin their comrades.

In one bomber, which came down behind the German lines east of the Meuse, the observer and airgunner tended the pilot of their machine for twenty-four hours, until he died. They then started to walk westward, contrived to pass the Meuse and reached a place of safety.

One officer who was brought down (wounded in two places) behind the German lines, set out westward and on his journey had to swim the Meuse twice (its course is much looped near Sedan). For some time he travelled with the enemy motor division, got away from them, reached the French lines and was sent by the French to hospital. The French Air Officer Commanding-in-Chief gave him the Croix de Guerre avec Palme.

During this battle, the enemy crossed the Meuse at several points between Givet and Namur, and broke through the French Ninth Army to a depth of fourteen miles west of Sedan.

It was said by the French President twelve days later that this Ninth Army was less well-officered and trained than other French armies, that the defences between it and the enemy were the poorest and the least solid, and that though it had a shorter road to march than the other armies, many of its divisions never reached their positions, so that it failed to take or to hold the important hinge-position given to it. The great enemy attack had fallen on "divisions scattered, ill-cadred and badly-trained for such attacks". Not all of it succumbed. During the next three days some remnants of it fought bravely here and there in the gap where they happened to be. But the army as an ordered force ceased to be; it was broken up. Some of the troops on the right of the First French Army shared the weight of the attack and the disaster.

That evening, when the Seventh French Army had been severely handled near Breda, and the Ninth French Army broken, the Dutch Army surrendered. This at once made it easier for the enemy to send greater strength against the French Seventh Army and the Belgians in front of Antwerp. Already the pressure on Louvain was increasing. At the end of the unhappy day, at the end of a stream of people leaving the city, an English writer saw the last of her citizens leaving, "a long train of nuns, at least a hundred, walking in twos to safety". There was to be no safety in Belgium.

The Sixth Day, Wednesday, 15th May.

The bombing of the ships in the Estuary of the Escaut and on the Dutch coast was always exceedingly severe; it also came with great violence upon the Seventh French Army in North Beveland and Welcheren. These troops, who were in no great strength and lacked artillery, were attacked by a picked enemy division, helped by the Fifth Column already in the islands; and driven out of the islands, back across the Flushing Ferry. It must be remembered that they were a weak detachment, unsupported as yet by artillery; they had outrun their supports. Their Light Mechanic Division fell back upon Antwerp.

On every part of their front the Allies were either falling back or preparing to do so. They were at all points pressed and at some points had had great loss. The sight of thousands of troops withdrawing upon Antwerp and Brussels, coupled with the knowledge that the Dutch had already surrendered, had a deplorable effect on the Belgian public. On this state of nerve, the enemy knew well how to play with rumour. It was on this day that the great exodus took place from the five chief cities in northern Belgium.

At the end of this day a soldier on the right of the British position, saw the remnants of a French Colonial battalion coming singly into our lines, broken and exhausted. In the distance, on the roads, he saw French horse-drawn transport moving towards the Lasne. They were not being molested, probably because the enemy had not yet brought up sufficient guns. At 10 p.m. the guns opened on these colurnns with a very heavy bombardment.

It was said in the army that the last aeroplane of the Belgian Army was brought down during this day.

At about 7 p.m. the enemy here and there broke through the French line south of Wavre, and as usual turned right and left from the point of the break to widen the wound. We took over some of the ground at the disputed point and restored the battle, though as it was not possible to restore the line, it was decided to fall back a little during that night to the line of the little river Lasne, two or three miles to the westward. The Lasne is but a brook; it has little cover on its banks and little water within them; it is even less of a tank obstacle than the Dyle.

All through this fighting the Royal Air Force fought with an heroic self-sacrifice, beyond all praise. In 171 sorties, they lost seventy-three aircraft. Eighty-seven of these sorties went to destroy bridges on the Meuse: forty aircraft were lost in this service: and of the twelve bridges attacked eight were destroyed or badly damaged. Unfortunately, the enemy had so many pontoon-trains and rubber-boats that the breaking of bridges seldom delayed him long. The Belgians asked: "Why should we destroy these costly and beautiful bridges, when the enemy will make a working bridge in less than a day?"

Three fighter squadrons of the Striking Force shot down seventy-four enemy aircraft in these six days, with a loss to themselves of sixteen. Some of our pilots were making three, four or five sorties a day, often at a great height, often in bitter battle: they had very little rest. Often after a hard day they would ask for a share of the work at night. Surplus crews sometimes used the same aircraft by day and night. The work of the salvage and maintenance men during this time was superb.

By the 17th, many of our fighter-pilots were utterly exhausted: the strain had been greater than it was again, until the last days of the evacuation.

The Seventh Day, Thursday, 16th May.

On this day the covering parties were embarked from Holland, and a number of British subjects taken away from Ostend. At Antwerp, the Navy had helped to get away from the port about eighty per cent of all the shipping in reach, amounting to twenty-six ocean-going ships. They had also secured all the dredgers, half the tugs and about 600 barges. As Antwerp could not be held, its oil-stores were destroyed. The light oils were set running into the fields; the 150,000 tons of other oil, including 70,000 tons of heavy oil, were fired. Nearly twenty-six years before, an immense cloud of black smoke from burning oil had been Rupert Brooke's last sight of Antwerp; similar bale-fire marked our going now.

The Seventh French Army was now being taken through the Belgian Army and sent to the south; the remains of one of its divisions, with reinforcements of other troops, kept near the East Flanders coast, with their left flanks guarded by our destroyers. The summer weather shone upon a sad scene of ruin. Belgium was already a broken land. Her armies were falling back; her roads were choked with the fleeing; the enemy was coming forward everywhere in greater strength than was there to meet him. In the sky, there were his multitudes of bombers, on the roads and in the lanes and coming over the fields were his hordes of tanks and motor-cyclists; he was coming with his three or four to one, all carefully trained in what they had to do; the power and the initiative were both his. The passing of news in our armies was extraordinarily difficult already. It was not until this day that the disaster to the Ninth Army was made clear. We learned now that the enemy was right through the Allied line on a wide front, and that all our right flank was in danger of being turned. Probably most of the armies on the Lasne and the Dyle supposed that there would be armies of reserve at Laon, Guise and Landrecies, ready to move up if needed, instantly. They did not imagine that this was not the case, nor that the enemy's multitude of bombers was making it impossible for the armies in reserve to take train to the danger-point. Something of the truth reached our commanders, who, throughout this campaign were very quick to perceive how very dangerous delay might be with such enemies as ours. In this forenoon, therefore, the British command asked for orders, and presently received word that the Allies would fall back,

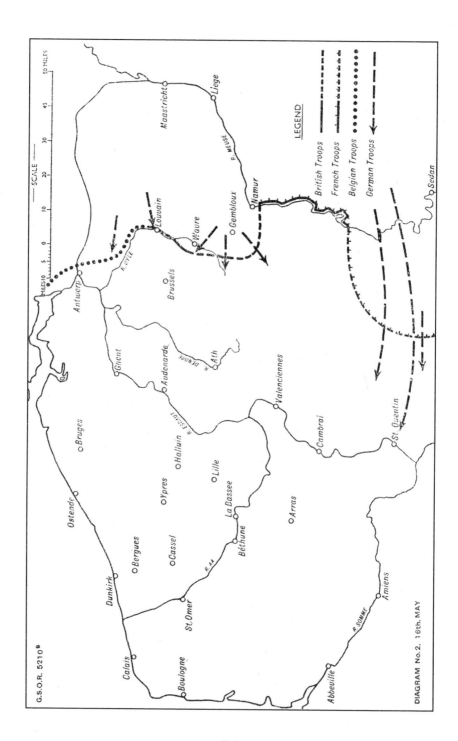

G.S.O.R. 5210 B

LEGEND

British Troops
French Troops
Belgian Troops
German Troops

DIAGRAM No. 2. 16th. MAY

76

starting that night, marching fifteen miles or so to the line of the Senne River, staying one day there; then falling back to the line of the Dendre River, delaying the enemy there, and on the 19th perhaps reaching the strong line of the Escaut. Preparations were made for this withdrawal; gear was loaded and despatched; bridges to our front were blown or prepared for it, and orders issued.

Though they were by this time far behind the enemy advance, like little islands in a German sea, the forts at Liege, under Colonel M. J. M. Modard, still held out as in the last war. The King of the Belgians spoke directly to Colonel Modard, calling him by name and saying, "Resistez jusqu'au bout pour la Patrie".

The retirement from the northern positions began at about five that afternoon, with the blowing up of two tons of dumped ammunition and petrol. Perhaps called by the explosion, eighteen Heinkels at once attacked the retiring company with bombs and machine-guns. Five of our Hurricanes at once came to the rescue, shot down eight and drove the other ten away. There were plenty of rumours of disaster to the French further south, "the enemy are through on the right and the French are melting away". The women enemy agents were noted as busy at the telephones, asking, "Who is there?" at houses likely to be used as headquarters. Those of our men who passed near Brussels heard the air-raid whistles blow their melancholy warning every few minutes. The roads were jammed with every kind of transport; the refugees in their misery going they knew not where, and soldiers trying to reach rendezvous across the drift. There were very heavy attacks on the left of the B.E.F., where the enemy motor-troops were filtering in. However, a hard fight held the enemy here, and though the rear-guards expected a rough night, in a bad position, the enemy was not swift to follow up in force. Here and there, he was already through in small detachments. Four soldiers who had been in the ruins of Wavre, loading a lorry, suddenly found German motor-troops in the road below them. They got away without their lorry and had to swim the Lasne. The town of Wavre, which had been a quiet little place a week before was now a smoking heap of desolation. The night march was of extreme difficulty; there was not much moon, the men did not know the country, there were a great many new roads through the beautiful forest south of Brussels, and many of these were not marked on our maps. The roads were so crowded with civilians without discipline that ordered movement was impossible. The tanks which ought to have been entrained had to come by road, because the engine-drivers had deserted; with tanks, guns, transport, refugees, an army and the relics of two other armies all moving on the same roads, the confusion was appalling and the march exceedingly fatiguing. In one wet place a pontoon-train completely blocked the way. Rumour was busy all the way that the enemy was through in the south, that he had sent parties of soldiers dressed as refugees, and that these had seized the bridges. There was a good deal of talk of parachutists and enemy agents; but gradually the strain of the march silenced even rumour. Some battalions marched thirty miles that day, without sleep.

The Eighth Day, Friday, 17th May.

They marched on when morning came, because the enemy light motor-troops were on the Nivelles road trying to forestall us at Hal. Troops on the left of the march opened fire to their left at 3.15, and sent out patrols who found no enemy. Everywhere, the march was fatiguing and confused. The cars and lorries of the units were mixed-up together. The drivers then made efforts to find their friends, hastened to catch up those who had passed or waited for those still to come and ever made the confusion greater. Reports came that the enemy light armoured cars were almost at Hal. These had come in between the B.E.F. and the First French Army, in a gap known to be at least two kilometres wide. The 48th Division marched to close the gap and to be the guard upon that flank. It had some hard marches in the seventy-two hours of the retreat, eighty miles in the three days, some reckoned, with little food and almost no sleep. Some of the men collapsed as they marched from utter exhaustion. All day long, the scenes on the road were heart-breaking. If our men were weary and hungry, the lot of the civilians was much worse. All day the armies marched by the fields in which the cattle had been left unmilked and often without water, and through villages left desolate. The deserted dogs began to attach themselves to the army.

A squadron of our bombers, sent out this day to help the French First Army, met with very terrible opposition near Gembloux. Only one, badly-damaged machine returned from this sortie.

The news from the south of the French frontier was exceedingly

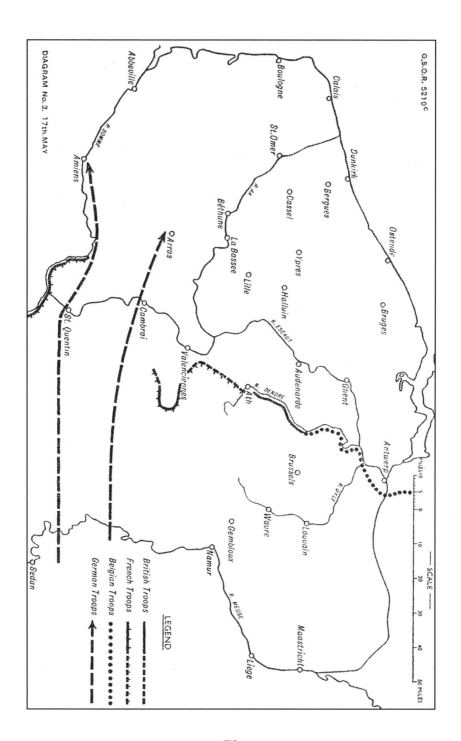

DIAGRAM No. 3. 17th MAY

LEGEND

British Troops

French Troops

Belgian Troops

German Troops

SCALE

MILES 10   5   0   10   20   30   40   50 MILES

grave; the enemy was now across the Oise, threatening St. Quentin. Reports said that he had ten armoured divisions in his army. It seemed likely that he was going to try to encircle all the Allied armies north of the French frontier. General Georges sent General Giraud to command the French troops now trying to check this German advance, General Giraud is a soldier of splendid presence and vigour. He is counted one of the best soldiers of France. Unfortunately, soon after his arrival in this part of the front, he was captured while making a first reconnaissance in a tank. Many feel that his capture at this critical time was a disaster to the French nation.

General Georges had still one good tank obstacle across the line of the enemy advance. This was the Canal du Nord, running, roughly speaking, southward from Douai and almost making a north and south line from Douai to the Somme by a junction with the river Tortille. General Georges ordered the 23rd British Division to occupy and hold this line.

This division was of less than half-strength. It consisted of eight battalions of infantry, without tanks or artillery. It had not yet completed its training, and had been employed since its arrival in France at work in the back areas. It gathered together what field, anti-tank and anti-aircraft guns could be had and moved to take up its position.

As the enemy was now threatening to cut the B.E.F. from all its southern bases, all the troops on the lines of communication were moved up to try to bar the way. These men were few in numbers, new to war, not yet fully trained, and with a weak equipment of artillery. They moved up, to guard Peronne and Albert, the bridge-heads keeping the Somme. Similar troops from our bases nearer home moved up from the sea to help in the defence of our threat-ened right flank, to break down certain bridges, guard crossings and improvise defences. A special body of men, known as "Mac Force" was placed between Douai and St. Amand. Such news as came through showed that the French efforts to close the gap in the line were coming piece-meal and unsuccessfully. The enemy's great strength in bombers made it impossible for the French to entrain their armies in time. The armies with the B.E.F.were still two days' march from the gap.

On this 17th May, the Belgian Government moved to Ostend.

The Belgian Premier visited King Leopold that afternoon. "Il l'a trouvée calme à l'armée." Late in the afternoon the Maire of Brussels surrendered his city to the Germans, who entered it. They also entered Malines, and what remained of Louvain. Small bodies of Germans had been in parts of Louvain for the last two days; the ruins were no longer disputed. They seem to have filled the enemy with pride.

The Ninth Day, Saturday, 18th May.

Our army was now falling back to the Escaut position; its left was still on the Senne, its centre mainly on the Dendre, and its right flank stretching between the two rivers. It had had and was having a weary withdrawal, on crowded roads, through ruined homes, among desolate and heart-broken people. The enemy bombers looked down on them, followed them and bombed them. In the want of exact knowledge of what was happening, rumour was ready to make it seem worse than it was. There was a general feeling that this was the day on which a big counter would be put in by French Armies moving northward from the Aisne. The troops had not yet begun to know how fatal a blow the enemy had struck. One of our men summed up the new kind of war thus: "War is more confused than ever, with everybody behind everybody's else's lines".

With this uncertainty of where the enemy might appear, the difficulty of getting news, for wires were cut almost as soon as laid, the expectation of treachery, the daily arrest of spies, the bombing, the universal misery of the women and children, came great fatigue, the want of proper supplies and a sense of confusion. It was one of those situations in which the people of these islands usually shine.

To most of the B.E.F. the 18th was a day of weary retreating; some lucky units had only short marches to make; most marched all day, in hot sunny weather with much wind, dust and blowing smoke. The smell of burning homes was never out of men's nostrils. Some units marched themselves to exhaustion and had to halt for rest. Not far from Ninove, the sniping and Fifth Column treachery became so dangerous, that the marching troops rounded-up all the civilians who could be found and kept them under armed guard. While this was being done, the snipers shot a number of women and children. In Ninove itself, all through this day, a three-abreast stream of traffic slowly loitered. At the end of the day the right flank expected a rest, but a little before midnight word came that the French on their flank were falling back behind the Escaut and that our men would have to conform. They got up to march back, and at midnight beyond the field of Fontenoy were caught in a traffic jam on a narrow bridge, which held up the advance for hours.

As the enemy was now in possession of Amiens, and pushing westward towards the coast, our troops and bases south of the Somme were shut from us. The French Armies to the south were unable to move northwards, to stop the Germans. We were unable to move south to stop them; We were now tied to the Belgians, engaged on the north, the east and the south, with forces superior to our own: all our bases were threatened, and our lines of communication in danger. All through the campaign these lines had been sorely harassed by bombers, now they were threatened by tanks as well; it was becoming difficult to supply our army with food, petrol and munitions. Already, our air force had been compelled to leave the French aerodromes and work from England. This made it exceedingly difficult for our fighter machines to be where they were most sorely needed. With the enemy moving fast westwards, and already forty miles round our right flank, with greater strength than our own, with the Belgian Army exhausted on our left, and the enemy attacking everywhere, it seemed likely, that we should have to retreat to some position near the sea, probably to the north of Boulogne, and hold a fortified camp there, if we could.

The exposed and dangerous right flank was strengthened in every possible way; the 23rd Division was withdrawn from the Canal du Nord to Arras, and the suggestion was made that possibly we might have to retreat to the coast "to a perimeter of which Dunkirk would possibly be the centre". During the evening, General Gamelin was removed from the command of the French Army; his post was given to General Weygand. A man who saw the track of the enemy advance writes that "for a stretch of twelve miles, at every ten or twenty yards, there was an auto-truck, tank or bus lying in the ditch". Most of these had been knocked-out and burned. "There were more than a thousand vehicles forsaken by their crews from Avesnes by Le Cateau towards Cambrai."

It may be well to consider the fortunes of a mixed body of

Territorials who set forth in the darkness in lorries before one o'clock on this morning to take position at the junction of the Canal du Nord with the Somme. They were a part of the forces hurriedly improvised to block, or attempt to block, the passage between the Somme and Arras. They expected that they would find support on their right from some French Army or group of armies moving up from the south.

They came to their ordered position. They could get no news of what was happening nor find any trace of French support on their right. The roads were still crowded with refugees; they saw French, Dutch and Belgian soldiers continually passing among the hordes. A section of French soldiers with an anti-tank gun offered to stay with them; and stayed for some four hours, but then moved on. When it was light an aeroplane attacked them with machine-gun fire. After this a party of about fifty men appeared. They wore civilian clothes, and looked like refugees, but it was noticed that they moved in military formation, and had a sort of uniformity; each carried a blanket in a roll. They were ordered back, but would not go till shots were fired over their heads.

Tanks were reported all through the day, but examination showed that the supposed tanks were refugees, vehicles, and, in one case, a horse.

As the light began to fail at about 8.30 that night, three tanks were indistinctly seen about 1,000 yards away. At the same time a vast cannonade broke out in the direction of St. Quentin, about fifteen miles away to the east-south-east. All hands were by this time very weary, having been on the roads for three days; they now received orders to withdraw to Albert, where they passed the night.

They went out into the Place of Albert in the morning of:

The Tenth Day, Sunday, 19th May.

During the forenoon they saw two large, low-flying enemy aeroplanes above the little Ancre River; it was supposed that they were dropping ammunition to their tanks. Presently a German motorcyclist was seen only fifty yards from the central square, probably on the Bapaume road; he was fired at, but escaped. Almost at once word came that thirty enemy tanks were advancing from the south-east and twenty more from another point. Almost at once a tank entered the square and opened fire, while a plane swooped down and joined in. "The noise was terrific and it was impossible to judge what was happening." Some survivors in a truck got out of the town to the north-west (evidently by the pleasant little chalk lane leading to Mesnil). On the rise, a mile from Albert, two little French boys cried "Les Allemands", whereupon a burst of fire came at them. They swung away at the cross-roads, full speed ahead, and were soon lost. "We came upon an enemy tank in a field with one of the crew sitting on the top having breakfast. I again said, 'Step on it,' and had a couple of shots at the German with a rifle. Machine-gun fire followed us, but we kept on going till we ended in a field. We had to risk turning back, but we dodged the tank. At last we found Doullens". The narrator adds that there were at least fifty tanks, light and medium, in this action, that the enemy probed to find the easy place, and left all strong points alone. He writes: "An anti-tank gun will kill one tank, after which the enemy will seek a softer spot. It is the enemy's doctrine that no weapon should fire more than three times from the same position. The refugees were the enemy's strongest ally, by stopping our mobility. I saw not one atrocity, but he controlled the confusion very cleverly by firing fore and aft of the columns".

By this time, forethought had done all that it could to guard what could be guarded with what there was. Mac Force had been gathered together and put on the line of the Scarpe, from Raches to St. Amand, with a gun at each bridge. Guards had been placed at points westward from the Canal du Nord at Albert, Doullens and St. Pol. A body known as Petre Force had taken position to defend Arras. On this 19th of May, Mac Force was reinforced and greatly extended, so that the line held by it ran westward to La Bassée.

The French First Army on the right of the B.E.F. were now heavily attacked from the air, with ground-support of the usual kinds, from tanks, mortars and artillery. The early morning brought heavy air attacks, on the crowded roads on all the operation areas. These attacks went on all day long, and probably killed more civilians than troops.

The fatigue of our troops on the right was so very great, that the last stage back to the line of the Escaut put many of them out of action. Transport was gathered for those who could not march, so that by the evening most of them were in position. Many of these men had been marching, fighting, or both, for a week; one battalion had been on outpost duty for seven nights in succession. Some sense of the state of the roads may be gathered from an artillery officer's note, that within and at the outskirts of a little Brabant town, where three main roads converge and become one, there was a traffic block seven miles long, luckily not seen by the enemy. This block had been like a revolving storm all the day before: now it had stopped. At one point, farther south, the transport of four divisions was moving on one road, three abreast, and head to tail. As soon as it was light, the bombers came on to this road, machine-gunned the drivers, bombed the lorries and set fire to them. Tournai was burning fiercely and deserted. Someone had opened the gates of the lunatic asylum here and released four hundred lunatics. These unfortunates added their share to the misery already present. When the refugees were here turned off the roads into the fields, a Signals Officer saw two enemy bombers come down, bomb and machine-gun them.

Already, the inmates of another large asylum had been set loose; the roads had at least a thousand mad men and women on them; how many went mad among their fellow-wanderers can never be known. Our soldiers were told to bring in mad people for examination, since some of the eccentric folk on the roads might be enemy agents. The medical officers examined a good many such cases; the genuine cases were released.

When the troops reached their positions on the Escaut, they set to work upon the position. All the barges were collected and drawn to the western bank, the trenches were dug, batteries protected, and lines established. The enemy was fast following upon our heels; the centre was under shell-fire at once, not heavy, nor well directed, but steady. Soon after our men had gathered the barges, the water in the Escaut began to fall, and fell rapidly between three or four feet. The sluices were somewhere in French or Belgian hands; our men could only suppose that the water had been drained away to make a protective inundation elsewhere. The result of the draining was that the barges were left grounded and the great central position of Belgium was no longer a real obstacle. By darkness, the army was on its line.

At Tournai, the enemy was pressing so closely upon our troops that it was judged better to blow the strong concrete bridge over the Escaut before his men could rush it. Major Rowland Willott,

D.S.O., R.E., went out under fire to the centre of the bridge to make sure of its destruction. He "lighted the safety-fuse before firing the electric circuit": but when returning to his side of the river "he noticed an old Belgian woman walking on to the far end of the bridge. He ran back under fire, carried the woman to safety, and then fired the bridge electrically with complete success".

While the army was settling to its new line, a meeting was held in London to "consider the maintenance of the B.E.F. through Dunquerque, Calais and Boulogne, and secondly, the possible evacuation, which was considered to be unlikely, through those three ports". Already, the problem of the lines of communication was beginning to be acute.

After this day, our aircraft were forced to work from bases in England.

The Eleventh Day, Monday, 20th May.

As we were now shut from the forces south of the Somme, our commanders could not combine attacks with our Allies beyond that river. It was clear, that if attacks had been made from the south they had been unsuccessful. It was possible that an attack by the B.E.F. and First French Army, aiming southward from Arras and Cambrai, might check the enemy's advance to the coast. Preparations were made for this attack, under very great difficulty. Both the armies about to attack were shut from their lines of supply and the bulk of their reserves. Their transport was subject to heavy bombing, and the line which they proposed to attack was elusive, moving all the time, dependent on no line, but always able to draw supplies and support from the air; there was no particular front, as in the last war. A front began wherever tanks found a place to attack. How strong the enemy was could not be certainly known; he was immensely strong; still, a move to the south across his track was certain to be annoying to him and might conceivably end his advance. Troops were moved and preparations made for an attack on the morrow.

While these were being made, the enemy high command gave a treat to the foreign correspondents with their armies. They took their guests to see "the ruins of Louvain Library". This library, once famous, had been completely destroyed by the Germans in 1914.

After the Great War it was rebuilt and restocked with books by the gifts of generous Americans; now it was again destroyed by the Germans. As one of the correspondents wrote: "Its 700,000 volumes must be considered lost"; however, he adds, "we had no reason to regret a slight loss in time, for what we saw was a human drama". What humanity there might be in the brutal destruction of learning and culture is not clear to us.

The enemy had many spies, sympathisers, helpers and agents among our positions behind the Escaut. At one village many of the inhabitants made organised resistance to us. In another a lamp-signaller was almost caught in an upper room in a church. He had used the place for some time, for he left behind him as he fled many burnt cigarettes, some food and the marks of long stay.

A little farther north nineteen enemy agents were convicted and shot; at one village, the Commanding Officer of a battalion was found dead in the road, having been shot in the back by a pistol.

That night all the bombers which could be spared went out in the clear moonlight to bomb the enemy in the Cambrai and Le Cateau districts in front of the French positions. It was hoped that on the morrow the English and French might advance southwards, and clear the roads before them.

The Twelfth Day, Tuesday, 21st May.

For six days, anxious people here had been wondering when a great effort would be made from north and south to close the gap through which the enemy was advancing. Speed was the enemy's successful weapon; a swift counter seemed called for. To the men on the spot, who were doing and suffering, to deliver a swift counter was not easy. The French First Army was in dificulties; it had been severely battered during the last week. The French armies south of the Aisne and the Somme were checked in their entrainments by an overwhelming bombing of trains and sidings. The B.E.F. was in a dangerous situation, becoming worse every moment, and needing every man and gun to protect its bases and turned right flank. Every movement of our troops was difficult, because of the immense strength of the enemy in the air and in swiftly-moving mechanical weapons. We had few aeroplanes, no great reserves of men, and few tanks. We, here, in safety, had thought that an attack by forty thousand men, half from the B.E.F., half from the First French Army attacking southwards, might meet a French Army pushing northward and so establish a position by this time exceedingly grave. When the time came, our army had not anything like twenty thousand men for the venture, nor had the French. Early in the morning, it was explained that the French main body could not attack until the next day or later. Still, the case was of extreme necessity; Frankforce attacked with what troops it had.

The battle has been described thus: "To the west of Arras, the 12th Lancers, a mechanical cavalry regiment, observed and reported enemy movements. To the east of Arras, on our left flank, were some weak elements of the French cavalry and two battalions of the 23rd Division, now finally withdrawn from the Canal du Nord. At six o'clock we were to attack round the west and south of Arras, with motor-cyclists ready to exploit any success towards Bapaume. The attack was in two columns, each with one tank battalion.

"The left column made progress, destroyed many cars, captured over 400 Germans and put the enemy tanks to flight.

"The right column began well, but . . . the enemy was in great strength; he had several batteries of field artillery and a complete air-superiority directing artillery fire on our slow-moving tanks. At 18.00 hours further progress was impossible. Troops halted, meaning to begin again next day. At 19.00 hours the enemy made a very severe bombing and machine-gun attack on the 1st Tank Brigade and infantry (with incendiary bombs on the tanks). The enemy tanks attacked at 20.00 hours and some of the infantry suffered heavy casualties; it was clear that the 1st Tank Brigade would not be fit for action by next day. The 12th Lancers reported that enemy columns with tanks were pushing towards St. Pol and threatening to turn the right flank." The troops held the ground which they had won until the morning.

This, which was meant to be a battle or sortie for liberty, became the first of the battles for Arras. By some unhappy error, M. Reynaud told the French Press this day that Arras had fallen; it was as yet only threatened.

The next day, the Press stated that the French had recaptured Arras.

At this time the enemy was making four great efforts:

1. To take Boulogne, which was now being heavily bombed.
2. To cut us from the sea by a thrust towards Bethune, Cassel, etc.
3. To break the French First Army, already sorely shaken near Valenciennes.
4. To complete the ruin of the Belgian Army.

In this fourth attack some observers this day noted that the enemy sent troops forward disguised as women, "in black clothes with yellow sashes".

To meet the second of the enemy efforts mentioned above a new body, known as Polforce, was swiftly improvised to guard our right flank as far as St. Omer.

During the six days of marching and fighting, with little rest, on crowded roads, subject to continual bombing, our Army's loss of motor vehicles, by breakdown or destruction, had been very great. The heavier lorries stood the strain fairly well, the lighter ones collapsed. The loss of ambulances, water-carriers, motorcycles and small transport generally, had become serious, for with these things went the stretchers, blankets and medical supplies.

During this day another meeting was held in England "to consider the emergency evacuation of very large forces, the necessity for air protection, and the need of a large number of small boats to carry troops to the off-shore ships". The need had not yet become urgent, but its possibility was plain, and by no means pleasant. "The emergency evacuation of very large forces" is the most difficult operation of war, Xerxes and Napoleon had tried it by land, with almost complete disaster. What they had failed to do by land, we might now be called upon to do by sea, from open beaches without cover, under an air force that reckoned itself master of the air, and in the presence of a swiftly-moving, exceedingly dangerous, well-trained and powerful army sworn to our utter destruction. Those who discussed the problem hoped that it might not be given to them to solve, but applied themselves to it. Already, some in England were beginning to speculate the chances of an emergency evacuation, and not reckoning them very high.

The Thirteenth Day, Wednesday, 22nd May.

Though Frankforce stood upon the ground it had won in the battle of the 21st its position was insecure. The enemy was bringing up a great mass of artillery and armoured vehicles from the direction of Cambrai. Under the threat of these, the French light cavalry on our left withdrew, and the battle for Arras drew nearer. All day long the threat to our lines of communication increased. Tanks in numbers were appearing at odd places as far west as St. Omer. Rumours of their presence were everywhere. By nine on this morning some elusive tanks were across all our communications at Arras. These came, saw, and disappeared. Presently, strong enemy forces attacked the line of the Scarpe to the east of Arras, and were held.

We were now moving troops westward from the Escaut to guard our right flank. Those who were going, mention less congestion on the roads, but always some trouble, either from refugees or from people who stayed at home and helped the enemy. In the centre of our main position on the Escaut all the many dogs which had attached themselves to a Signals Office, where they were fed, were ordered to be destroyed, as it was very hot and there was little water. An enemy bomber was brought down here in flames. Many French men and some of ours ran to the wreck; its bombs exploded ten minutes later and wounded two. "No man approached a fallen plane after this." On the Canal that night the solid pack of grounded barges was fired, so that the sky was lit up for miles. In the evening some enemy machines approached under cover of a crowd of refugees; some rifle grenades were sent at them, they then withdrew. In the darkness of that night, for though it was full moon it was raining a little, two stalwart Scotchmen in a car moving westward to the new positions pulled out of the line of transport and tried to cut in ahead. The C.O. of a battalion stopped them with a rope of oaths ("our Army swore terribly in Flanders"), but when he learned that they belonged to a battalion which had done valiant service beside his own the day before he sent them on with his blessing.

On this day some Royal Marines and two battalions of Guards prepared Boulogne for defence, for the enemy was now there, and flowing on towards Calais. At about eleven o'clock that night the battle for Boulogne began.

The Fourteenth Day, Thursday, 23rd May.

The Allied position now looked upon the map like a long index-finger pointing south-eastward from Dunquerque towards Sedan. The finger-tip, the First French Army, about Valenciennes, was too far forward for safety. It was shut from all its sources of supply, and looked as though it might be snipped clean off the finger. All the northern side of the finger held by the Belgian Army was in a dangerous condition and likely to collapse in the near future. The southern side was threatened everywhere, and a sharp axe-head seemed poised to cut the finger off at its root.

Already the effect of this axe-head was felt throughout the B.E.F. Our ports of supply were shut from us. The enemy had taken Abbeville, cut the line of the Somme, invested Boulogne and Calais, and was so bombing Dunquerque that the port could not easily be used. Some of our supplies were already short and uncertain; we had petrol, though we had lost much mechanical transport; we had not much food, nor very much ammunition. In some divisions regular rations could not be issued. In others, nearer to some great magazine of stores, matters were happier. We were short of artillery ammunition, especially of the heavier sorts. The enemy's great superiority in day-bombers made it impossible for us to bring up supplies by air, in the manner so cleverly performed by him in all the forward areas. As we shortened the line on this day, by a drawing back from the Escaut, so we shortened the issues to the troops.

There was exasperating confusion on the roads whenever our motor transport mingled with the French horse-drawn transport.

Our garrisons were very strongly attacked on the line of the Scarpe river in a determined battle for the possession of Arras, a famous and once beautiful city, which had suffered pretty thorough destruction in the last war.

The battle began at nine in the morning with a series of tank attacks to the north and west of the city along the railway line from St. Pol. The enemy captured a suburb at this point and was driven from it by our troops. Later, he attacked to the east of the town, to keep our men from helping the French still farther to the east, and also to complete the isolation of the city. The French light division cavalry which had been upon our front withdrew; our much-diminished tanks put in a counter-attack. During the afternoon it

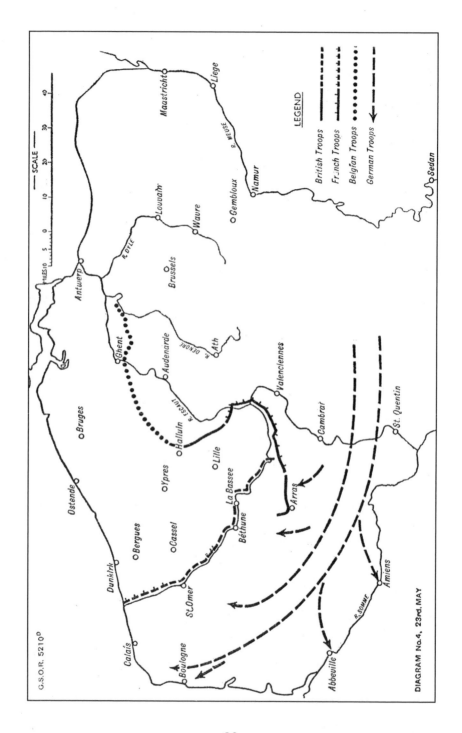

G.S.O.R. 5210^D

SCALE

LEGEND

British Troops

French Troops

Belgian Troops

German Troops

DIAGRAM No. 4, 23rd. MAY

92

was known that the enemy had reached the road directly north of Arras (leading to Bethune).

Arras was burning fiercely in many places; it was under continual dive-bombing; and very frequently, during the day, bodies of enemy troops, in one disguise or another, attacked our men from within the streets. The enemy seemed to have endless supplies of men on all the roads leading to the town. From 2 p.m. he began to try to cross the Scarpe. He brought up a bridging-train, which our guns destroyed. His infantry then began to come forward in waves, bringing light boats and bridging material. As always, the enemy persisted in this endeavour with the utmost devoted courage. "The Bren guns were not able to fire fast enough to cope with the masses of Germans." As there were not enough Bren guns, the enemy got across the Scarpe at about 8 p.m. and at the same time attacked Givenchy north-north east from the town. The garrison was now almost completely cut off. Word came that enemy tanks were attacking Lens. This could only mean that he was there in great force. Still, the battle for Arras went on till after midnight, when word came that the city was to be evacuated. It was three in the morning before the survivors left, and in their going they had a stroke of luck which they badly needed. They were leaving by the Douai, or eastern road, and found that the bridge over the Scarpe close to the city had been blown up. A party got across the Scarpe, but were at once captured by the enemy, who were in strength on the northern bank. The rest of the force turned northwards by the Henin road, which was the only exit not in enemy hands. They left the city by this road. Though the night was fine and the waning moon was still large, they were not bombed upon the way, but some of them (the 17th Infantry Brigade) had to fight a running rearguard action for some miles during the rest of the night; some of its detachments ran into parties of the enemy after daylight and suffered casualties. It was felt by the troops that the Germans would have captured Lens that night, if they had only pressed their attack after dark. Probably the enemy was as nearly exhausted by his efforts as we by ours.

The day was otherwise of great importance in the campaign. We lost Arras; we reduced rations; we shortened the line; we retreated; there was, moreover, an important council in Ypres. When leaving this, General Billotte, who had been active as a coordinator of the

Allied Armies, was wrecked in his motor-car and died soon afterwards. On this day, also, a telegram urged all commanders to put in force the plan made by General Weygand, now the French Commander-in-Chief, on the 20th.

This plan, which had been partly tried by the B.E.F. on the 21st at Arras, and by the French First Army that morning at Douai, was now known as the Weygand Plan. It was that the B.E.F. and the First French Army should attack with about eight divisions towards the south-west, with Belgian mechanical cavalry on the right. As these thrust south-west, a "Third French Army Group" was to attack northwards from Amiens to Peronne. Mechanical French cavalry was to advance with this army, having a British armoured division on its left.

Unfortunately, it was now difficult to put this plan in force. Our force at Arras was heavily engaged and being driven back; the French had been driven back; we were unlikely to receive help from the Belgians; we had very little ammunition; our tanks, both French and British, had lost heavily, had been much knocked about, and could not be replaced; nor was there any certain tidings that the "Third French Army Group" really existed.

An attack to the south was likely to be helpful; but as matters were it could not be immediate. Troops, guns and munitions had to be brought to the south for such a battle. Our command suggested that the battle should be fought on the 26th. But where were the troops to be had? Not from the north; our army there, pressed by the enemy, kept the sensitive point, where the Belgian Army joined ours. Not from the centre; the enemy there was pressing our men. Certainly not from the south; where the line, nearly sixty miles long, was in imminent danger of ruin. Certainly not from England; because our last remaining port in France was being so bombed that the harbour appliances, cranes and so forth, could hardly be used in daylight. Men might conceivably be landed on the beaches there, but their guns, transport and heavier munitions could not. As it was, all our Army's supply of bread, meat and ammunition had to be landed on the beaches and the system was not working very well. Certain states of wind and tide might interrupt it for days at a time.

On this day many of the B.E.F. must have wondered whether those beaches would not soon be in the enemy's hands. All our long, thinly-held right flank was threatened. Though most of the attacks were from tanks and mechanical cavalry, lots of field-guns had been brought up against us, and the infantry was being hurried forward. Boulogne was invested. Calais was cut off. Some of the armoured divisions which had shut up these towns were moving on Bethune, St. Omer and Gravelines to shut us from the sea and complete our ruin.

However, they had not yet cut us off, and efforts were being made to stop them. Much could be done to secure the threatened flank.

A good defensive line existed in a network of canals and drainage works which stretches from the sea to St. Omer. From St. Omer to the Escaut this line is continued by the La Bassée Canal. The line is about eighty miles long, and a part of it, the seaward part, is so broken with water-courses as to be difficult country for tanks. We had not enough men to guard this long line. All the men who could be scraped together to destroy its bridges and draw its boats and barges to the northern side were so employed. The greater number of the bridges were broken down or mined for blasting. As the advancing enemy columns came by the roads wherever and whenever they could, the better roads leading to this line were obstructed, broken, and in some cases mined or trapped.

The small mixed force, known as "Polforce", was placed on the line of the Aire and La Bassée Canals; a still smaller force, the now shattered and very weary 23rd Division, with the Green Howards, took over the line towards the sea. Some of the French fortress troops from this sector of France moved into position with them. They were hardly on the lines, holding them lightly with the few men to be had, when the enemy tanks with lighter vehicles appeared, and the fight for the line began.

The bombing was very severe throughout this day. The three coast towns of Boulogne, Calais and Dunquerque were severely bombed at intervals all through the day. The troops at Arras and Douai had endured heavy bombing throughout the fighting there. The enemy bombing force was so strong that even with all these drains upon it, dozens of bombers were at work elsewhere. As our men moved westwards, one man noted: "Lille seemed deserted (a city, usually, of more than 200,000 inhabitants) and the ruins showed the intensity of the air-attacks". Our once busy aerodrome at Seclin was ruined and deserted. The enemy bombers seemed to be everywhere; a man counted twenty-five at one time "bombing towns and villages". Apart from the bombing, the march was not molested; the enemy was not following very closely. Some lucky men, rummaging in a deserted truck in a railway siding, found that it contained chocolate. Perhaps this welcome find was the most cheerful event on that gloomy day. During the night the enemy dropped leaflets advising our men to surrender, as they were surrounded.

Perhaps the gloomiest thought which came into many men's minds on that day was the knowledge that thenceforward we had no landing-ground in Northern France for any aeroplane. This was no great disadvantage to our bombers; but very serious for our fighters, with short radius of action. Any aeroplanes needed had to be called, either by wireless message or telephone, from a base in England. The enemy had now the power to watch and bomb our movements with the almost certainty of finishing his work before our fighters could interfere.

BOULOGNE

Boulogne is familiar to many thousands of Englishmen to whom
it has been the gateway to the Continent. For four anxious years in
the Great War it was a populous English city, through which at least
half a million of our race passed to death for France. Not less than
a million others were shipped back wounded thence.

Boulogne consists of a lower and an upper town. The upper town
is, in the main, an old citadel, now planted about with trees. This
stands on the summit of a swell or ridge of chalk downland. The
lower town, partly on the slope of the chalk and partly on the low-
lying ground at its foot, is, or was before its capture by the enemy,
an important and growing sea-port. The entrance to this port is
curving and narrow; it can be very difficult in some weathers and at
certain states of the tide. Like most French coastal towns, Boulogne
had forts here and there near it, permanently garrisoned. Two of
these are at the northern end of the city.

The harbour has been skilfully adapted from the mouth of the
River Liane. It cuts the lower town in two; it is bridged by two
bridges and the railway by which so many Englishmen have passed
to Paris.

On 21st May the rapid advance of the Germans made it necessary
for us to reinforce Boulogne. That night two battalions of the Brigade
of Guards and some Royal Marines were ordered to proceed thither
at once with ten anti-tank guns. An air-raid warning sounded while
the men were embarking from England; the stores and equipment
had to be put on board in the dark. There were, of course, already
other troops in the city, both French and English, though many of
these were exceedingly weary men. As the port had been a very busy
base for the B.E.F., it had within it still some hundreds of Lines-of-
Communication men, pioneers and hospital units. For some days
before this the enemy had bombed the place frequently.

The reinforcements from England arrived early in the morning of the 22nd May. On arrival, one battalion, the Irish Guards, moved out to take up a position on the right, covering the south of the town from the outer breakwater to the River Liane, a front of about two miles in all.

The other battalion, the Welsh Guards, covered the east and north sides of the town, especially the roads to the bridge (Pont de Briques) over the Liane and the roads leading north to Calais. This made a front of three and a half miles.

As Boulogne lies at the foot of a rather abrupt slope it is difficult to defend. Some destroyers lying out at sea watched the flanks of the defending force.

In the afternoon the enemy appeared on the high ground to the south of the British positions. He was coming on in strength with tanks and field-guns. His main attack was to be from the south, because from that point the "Old Fort", or the suburb called Le Portel, he could shoot directly down into town and harbour. The garrison troops had made what preparations they could for defence. They had made road-blocks on the important roads with lorries, tree-trunks and blastings up of the surface. At 3.30 the enemy began to shell our positions. At 5.30 he made a tank attack. One tank was knocked out after receiving seven direct hits. At 6.15 the enemy made another attack with tanks under a cloud of aeroplanes. He overran one forward post and cut off a platoon of another company. At 10 p.m. there was more shelling and a vigorous attack with much confused fighting. It was very difficult for communications to pass, as the civil telephone service was now out of action. While this battle was going on just outside the city, one exhausted soldier in Boulogne notes: "In spite of every kind of noise, I couldn't keep awake for more than two minutes at a time and the men lay like logs".

At 1.55 in the morning of the 23rd, a destroyer drew into the quay to collect wounded. "The pier was like a shambles with the multitude of wounded and more were being brought down continually."

At 7.30 a very heavy shelling from guns and mortars began. Enemy tanks moved forward, and the advanced company of the Irish Guards had to be withdrawn. It had been fighting the enemy for two hours at a range of only thirty yards. The battalion took up a new line along the light railway which leads to the docks. The attack became heavier and the battalion had to fall back through the streets. Parties of the enemy were now creeping into houses here and there and firing from the windows with machine-guns. One English captain was heard raging and storming because he couldn't wake his men, though the enemy was in the next street. However, nothing will wake the completely exhausted.

While the Irish Guards were sheltering from heavy shelling in the houses at the sides of the road, some enemy tanks passed right through the position and then turned back towards the south again.

Meanwhile, as it was clear that the town could not be long held, the navy prepared to make certain demolitions and to evacuate the garrison. Some marines, engineers and naval ratings set forth from England to do this work. As they arrived they found the coast patrolled by French and English destroyers giving heavy and accurate fire upon tanks and armoured cars now coming towards the city from the north. A heavy attack had begun that morning upon the position of the Welsh Guards, who were put under artillery fire of much intensity. Their road-blocks had been set on fire, but they had driven the enemy back. He was now coming forward again.

Entering the harbour under heavy shell-fire, the demolition parties set about their work. The French had asked that certain things should be destroyed, the chief of these were: the power-house and pumping station, the lock-gates and swing-bridges, the cranes and harbour equipment, the floating dock and any shipping in the harbour likely to be useful to the enemy. A drifter in the port seemed too good to destroy. The naval ratings raised steam in her at once by a fire "of bits of packing-cases and anything combustible".

While charges were being laid in the works to be destroyed the enemy suddenly opened fire on a destroyer lying in the harbour. Parties of Germans with machine-guns had crept into a warehouse only a hundred yards from her starboard beam. The destroyer swiftly opened fire on the warehouse and blew it up. She then shelled the enemy in a fort on the north of the town and blew that up too.

The position of our men on both sides of the town was now uncertain and very dangerous. On the left bank of the river our troops held the Quai, the Douane, the three bridge-heads and the Gare Maritime. On the right bank the Welsh Guards were now withdrawing, but still held an irregular line from about the Holy Trinity Church to the Calvaire and Casino. A good many English troops were sheltering in the shrubbery or "small wood" in the Casino Garden. The enemy were roughly everywhere to the south, the east and the north. Tanks and guns were shelling us from three sides and many men who had filtered through into the town were sniping and machine-gunning from close at hand. Our men blocked the city roads against tanks, by carts and lorries. One man spent some time filling 200 empty wine and beer bottles with petrol. These things, when fused and lit, were to be flung at the tracks of tanks, if they broke through any barricade. (These weapons are called Russian cocktails, or tank destroyers.)

At about three that afternoon, two destroyers came in to load wounded and take away troops. They began to take in some of the men holding the northern defences. The men were told to creep from the shelter of the Casino Garden to pinnaces, which ferried them across the dock to the ship.

While this was being done in comparative quiet, between 60 and 100 bombers came over to upset the work. At the same time German troops from the northern heights opened a very heavy rifle and machine-gun fire, which killed the Captain of H.M.S. *Keith*. A pinnace-load of men returned from the Quai to the Casino Garden at this time with word that the evacuation order was cancelled. This was a mistake, it was not cancelled, only delayed till the light was a little less clear and movement of troops somewhat safer. To the men in the Casino Garden, it must have seemed almost like sentence of present death. "Not one comment was heard from the men, they just remained completely dumb. The officers made a rather faint-hearted attempt to laugh the situation off. When in doubt, a meal is the best thing to try. A ration lorry was near-by (whether by fore-thought or accident I cannot tell); food was distributed, and Captain Gibbs talked someone into producing hot water for the finest cup of tea on record. We had just finished when things really did start happening. At least thirty enemy bombers approached from Calais. They were set upon by British fighters and three went down in flames. Four got through and dive-bombed the Quai. Repeated attacks were driven off by the destroyers' A.A. fire, but a good few hits were scored. (Surprisingly few casualties.)" After this the fire became furious; the enemy brought up more guns, the destroyers replied, paying much attention to the tanks trying to enter the town from the north, and causing them much loss. One destroyer broke up three. The men in the Casino Garden kept under cover of the trees. In the harbour, the demolition parties, helped by fire from the destroyers, sank the floating dock, wrecked the cranes, and burst off the hinges of the sluices. They were also preparing to wreck the three bridges when the time came. The enemy were skilfully moving into the town, firing from upper windows and moving from house to house, always creeping nearer. The main garrison was now retreating to the Gare Maritime (some of which still stood) to embark on the two destroyers. This they did with great difficulty, under very heavy fire and close-quarter fighting. "In addition, great difficulties were caused by small parties and broken units of Belgians and French passing through the line and opening fire in various directions on their own."

At 7.20 the embarkation continued. "The Welsh Guards came down in complete quietness and good order. The quiet discipline of the Irish Guards and the steady bearing of the seamen and marines was really fine." They had had an exhausting and trying time. The fire from the destroyers passed over the heads of these men, and made it possible for them to embark in fair security. It must be remembered that the destroyers' guns' crews were out in the open, in full view of every German in the position; they stood to their guns and kept down the enemy fire till their ships were loaded. With occasional lulls, air-raids, and bursts of fire, the time passed till 8.25, when the two loaded destroyers put to sea. Three more were ready to take their place directly they left, but one of these took the ground at the entrance and was set on fire by incendiary shells. The two coming in were fired at from close range, for at the moment one enemy tank was moving down the Quai directly to her. This tank was hit by a shell from the destroyer and set on fire. The troops in the Casino Garden were now told to make their way round to the ships by the bridges. The lower town was burning in many places and so full of smoke that there could be little accurate shooting. The men crossed the river and embarked. It was low water. The destroyers lay fifteen feet below the Quai, and some men, in clambering down, fell in, and had to be fished out.

The coming in of the destroyers was remarkable.

H.M.S. *Venomous* was coming alongside under very heavy fire from rifles and machine-guns on the north of the town and from light field-guns from a battery in Fort de la Creche.

"Sub-Lieutenant W. R. Wells, R.N., got a wire ashore single-handed and made the destroyer fast. Then the *Venomous* opened fire on Fort de la Creche and blew down the side of it, sending guns and mountings rolling down the slope. Motor cyclists and a car came out of the main street towards them, but the *Venomous's* machine-guns scattered these. There was a terrific noise, but the embarkation went on. The *Venomous's* machine-guns caught an enemy column filing down a path and she brought down a wall and houses right on top of them. A field-gun fired on her among some trees in a garden, but a salvo blew the trees and the gun away. In these operations she fired off her complete outfit of ammunition and, being now filled with troops, she backed out of the narrow entrance. At this point her wheel jammed, but she managed to steer by her engines. The *Wild Swan* followed; she grounded in the shallow water, but got off. They took up H.M.S. *Venetia,* which was grounded just off the harbour. The noise was appalling. By this time the bridges had been blown and the other demolitions completed.

"It was now 21.27 hours. H.M.S. *Windsor* went in at 22.30 hours; she loaded up and went out astern. She was so loaded that there was not standing room. She was clear at 23.20 hours. At 1.30 on the 24th H.M.S. *Vimiera* got to the outer jetty. The silence was eerie; there was a burning lorry on the quai and a full moon; otherwise the harbour was dark. One British soldier stood on the jetty. Lieutenant Hicks hailed; and then there came word that there were more than 1,000 men still to be fetched off, including Belgians, French and refugees, as well as English. These began to come down on board and officers kept on saying 'Hold on another twenty minutes while we fetch our men'. At 22.30 she was crammed and could not get any more in. She had to leave 200. Five minutes later the shore batteries opened. She was the last to leave Boulogne and she had taken on board her 1,400 men. She was so packed that she was in a very dangerous condition. Her ship's crew's behaviour had been magnificent."

In all, these destroyers saved 4,368 men; many hundreds of them wounded. The last record-load at low water might very well have driven the ship so down into the mud that she would never have been able to move.

The Fifteenth Day, Friday, 24th May.

The enemy, having taken Boulogne and isolated Calais, now prepared to cut us off from Dunquerque. They began to drive their tanks on a broad front along the Aire Canal, which was the main defence of our sensitive flank. They tried their usual plan, of finding a weak spot and breaking through it. They crossed the canal at various points and at once made bridgeheads of their crossings. Very little success here would suffice to ruin us, by shutting us from the sea, our way of supply and of escape. It was imperative that we should not be cut off, surrounded and destroyed. This threat had to be met.

There was no chance, now, of forcing a passage to the south, to join the talked-of, but shadowy Third Group of French Armies supposed to be advancing to meet us. Our one hope, was to stop the Germans from cutting right across our rear, and to stop them at once, if we could.

Throughout this weary day our men marched to the places vital to the defence of the shaken flank, Bergues, Cassel, Wormhoudt, Hazebrouck, Merville, Bethune, and the hamlets between them.

One infantryman, passing through a little place called Aubers, about ten miles west-south-west from Lille, saw "many hundreds of refugees lying about dead". On the way, a good many enemy agents or sympathisers sniped at the troops; this was a feature of the march. There was constant bombing from the air. Some of the battalions were very short of supplies. One such arrived at one this morning to try to hold the Nieppe Canal, which makes a sort of outer moat to the vital town of Hazebrouck. The bridge at Steenbecque and the crossing at La Motte were vital to the holding of Hazebrouck. The enemy soon attacked with tanks, probing round the flanks and on the front; our divisional light tanks engaged them until about 3 p.m., when they could do no more against such weight of metal. The enemy followed up his advantage, drew near to Steenbecque and raked the place with machine-guns; they set some of the houses on fire. However, on its way to that point, the battalion had passed by our old aerodrome at Merville, and had there collected some weapons; three Lewis guns and a battery of Browning guns. None of the battalion "had ever fired any of these weapons on the range"; they did so now, with very good effect. They fell back from

Steenbecque, but continued to hold Morbecque, with a left flank in the Nieppe Forest at La Motte. "The mosquitoes in the forest were very vicious." Enemy tanks, as well as mosquitoes were there. However, that approach to Hazebrouck was held.

The Sixteenth Day, Saturday, 25th May.

This battalion still held its position, having, as rations for the whole battalion, four tins of biscuits and seven pounds of sugar. In the evening it received a telegram from its Divisional General, saying: "If you had not held the Steenbecque bridge against tanks and infantry for 48 hours the Boche might now be in Dunquerque".

During the night of the 24th–25th, the enemy, with a strong force, attacked the Belgian Army between Menin and Desselghem and broke it in on a wide front, just where a collapse would make a retirement of the whole Belgian line inevitable. The breaking of the Belgians here threatened our left, and made it highly likely that our way to the sea, already threatened from the south, would be cut off by an advance from the north on Ypres. Any enemy movement on Ypres would close our way to the sea to one very narrow corridor. If we were so closed the enemy bombers would concentrate upon the roads, the French First Army would be shut up and forced to surrender, and very few of the B.E.F. would escape.

Preparations were made to defend Ypres in case of need. The enemy continued to press his advantage against the Belgians; word came that he was preparing a big attack upon them in their positions on the Lys. Our only reserves were one regiment of machine cavalry and the two divisions held for the attack under the Weygand Plan. As the threatened attack upon Ypres might bring us to complete disaster, these divisions were held for the defence of Ypres and our left. It had begun to appear to observers that the Belgians could not long continue in the war. The possibility of their surrendering suddenly was present in our commander's mind. If they did so surrender, or were forced to some northward movement leaving our left flank open, our ruin might follow. It was imperative that we should take instant steps to lessen the ruin it would bring.

The first task, after putting a strong guard on the Ypres–Comines Canal, was to shorten the line.

Troops moving to the Ypres–Comines position found that civilian control had now completely broken down; there was no food supply for the population. In Ypres the ever-heroic nuns and Belgian Red Cross people were working the crowded hospitals, though starving. Our own army was moving upon one half, or even one third, rations; we could do little to help. By good fortune and good management the position on the Ypres–Comines Canal was occupied by our troops. It was by no means a strong position, for the water in the canal had almost gone; the sluices had been tampered with and an infantryman could ford it almost anywhere. Our men took up positions for what came to be called the Battle of Wytschaete from the village about the centre of the position.

During this day the enemy cut or bombed out of action the water-works which supplied Dunquerque. There were still a good many wells in the district, but by this time many canal sluices thereabouts had been opened to make inundations on the west and south of the city. These floods in a day or two made the ground sufficiently soft to check tanks. Unfortunately, by that time the water began to seep into all the wells and make them brackish. This was to add a good deal to the troubles of the B.E.F. before very long.

In the evening of this day the German High Command announced to the foreign newspaper correspondents with its armies that "the ring around the British, French and Belgian Armies has been definitely closed".

The Seventeenth Day, Sunday, 26th May.

On the Ypres–Comines Canal our troops prepared for a battle which could not long be delayed. They took up a lightly-held position along the Canal, facing north-east, with their right flanks guarded by machine-guns on the banks of the canal near Warneton. The powerful supports of two infantry brigades were on the slightly higher ground of Wytschaete. While waiting for the attack to begin, some units were told to break up their mechanical transport, and serve as infantry. The engines of the cars were ruined, or holes broken in the axle-casings.

Before noon the enemy began to test the position for a possible weak spot; the line was bombed, shelled and mortared. Patrols pushed along it to discover what lay in front of them, and then withdrew to let the shelling prepare an attack. As the attack was likely to be powerful, more troops and guns were ordered up to the defence. As usual, they found movement difficult from civilians, refugees, and drifting transport.

While this attack impended the enemy showed that he still hoped to cut us off from the sea. He was attacking, crossing and making bridgeheads upon the big canal which guarded our right flank to the sea. This canal is called, in different reaches, the Canal de la Colme, the Canal de l'AA, the Aire Canal, etc. To the B.E.F. it was the right flank. We had one battalion on the sea at Gravelines. Next to this came some battalions of a remaining division of the French Seventh Army in and near Dunquerque. For the rest of the line, we had parts of three divisions of the B.E.F. trying to hold Hazebrouck, Cassel, Wormhoudt and Bergues. The French First Army was being plucked westward from its dangerous advanced position, but it was still too far out, and being hotly attacked. To many soldiers it seemed likely that the German announcement, though false for the moment, might soon prove to have been prophetic.

On this day our Government learned that no French Army or group of armies could advance from south of the Somme to engage the enemy.

A telegram was sent to the British Commander-in-Chief, saying: "In the circumstances no course is open but to fall back upon the coast. You are now authorised to operate towards coast forthwith in conjunction with French and Belgian Armies."

Some authorities in London at that time thought that if we were lucky we might possibly succeed in getting away 30,000 men in all; the rest would be lost. In times of great danger, this people sometimes rise above expectation. At 6.57 this evening the preparations made for evacuating troops from Dunquerque were put into active practice: some of the men at the base were removed to England, and the beach-parties arranged for more to follow soon.

Very heavy enemy bombing went on all this day; with the bomb a great many ill-written leaflets were dropped. They read as follows:

"Germans around. You are encircled British soldiers. Calais will be taken immediately. Why do you fight further? Do you really believes this nonsens that Germans kill their prisoners? Come and see yourselves the contrary. The match is finished. A fair enemy will be fairly treated."

The match was not quite finished.

On this day, during a heavy bombing, Dunquerque's oil-tanks were set on fire. From this time the troops of the B.E.F. had before them as they marched a pillar of fire by night, a pillar of cloud by day.

During this evening, preparations were made at many points to defend the sensitive right flank between Hazebrouck and Bergues. At all the important towns between these places, a defence had been improvised. In between the towns, small parties of men with a few guns and Lewis guns, took up defensive positions to delay the enemy as much as possible. The defence of this right flank with insufficient troops and guns was one of the great feats of the campaign. At Hondeghem, a village between Hazebrouck and Cassel, the positions were held by four field-guns and a detachment of thirty men, with nine or ten Bren guns and two anti-tank rifles.

Two of the field-guns were posted to command the roads leading from the west: the Bren guns were placed in upper windows. The enemy was known to be in force a few miles away; the defenders could quite certainly count on being attacked next morning by an overwhelming might of tanks. Their own hope of reinforcement was slight. What was done at Hondeghem was being done at twenty other little places by detachments as small and as determined. Some day the full story of these Thermopylae will be told. They foiled the enemy's main effort, which was, at that moment, to break the right flank and shut us from the sea.

CALAIS

CALAIS is nearer to us than any other town on the Continent. It can frequently be seen from the English coast, being only about twenty-one miles distant. It must be almost as well known to English people as Boulogne.

Like Boulogne, it consists of an old and a modern city. Canals and branches of the harbour make both cities islands linked by numerous bridges. The old city is dominated on its western side by the fortress of the citadel, which, like other citadels in France, was held by a garrison of French soldiers.

When it became clear that the town was threatened by the German advance, the city garrison was reinforced from England by the Rifle Brigade, a battalion of the 60th Rifles, a battalion of Queen Victoria's Rifles, and a battalion of cruiser tanks of the Royal Tank Regiment, under Brigadier-General C. Nicholson. These troops were landed on the 22nd May, with eight anti-tank guns.

The town had already been repeatedly and heavily bombed. The tanks, moving out to the south-west on landing, met posts of the enemy on the roads leading from Boulogne.

During Thursday, 23rd May, the Queen Victoria's Rifles set a company to guard the approaches from Dunquerque, and then took position to the west of Calais, towards Sangatte. The 60th Rifles and Rifle Brigade took position in a half-circle outside the south and the east of the town.

At dawn on Friday, 24th May, the patrols met the enemy. The fight which then began continued through the day. At 11 that morning, the Scotch ship *Kohistan* left Calais, with many wounded and refugees. Her Master made the following note: "When leaving Calais, men of the Rifle Brigade were lined up alongside the station, and waved and cheered us, although they knew they were left to certain death."

The outer defences of the town were held until nightfall of the 24th, when all our troops fell back towards the old town and Fort Risban at the harbour entrance. The French still held the citadel. The petrol tanks were now blazing; enemy infantry, creeping down the approaches, were attacking from the south and west. Our ships, standing-in, shelled whatever enemy could be seen. Some ships came into the port and took away wounded and various base units. The Commanding Officer told the sailors that a recent counter-attack had re-established his line, but that his troops were tired and had not much ammunition left.

Had the campaign elsewhere been favourable to us, the troops would have been taken from Calais that night. As it happened, the enemy was making such an effort to cut us from Dunquerque that any action which delayed some of his army was of priceless advantage. After 11 that night a signal was sent to the Commanding Officer saying: "Your role is to hold on. The R.A.F. will drop ammunition. You will select the best position and fight on."

On Saturday, the 25th, the enemy increased the strength of his attacks. It was supposed that he had received reinforcements of tanks and of infantry. Orders were sent to the garrison that the defence must continue, since every hour of delay to the enemy was of the greatest help to the B.E.F. Between three and six in the afternoon at least forty guns were shelling our position. The shelling was so heavy that no ships could enter the harbour. It was reckoned that the losses of the defenders were by this time up to sixty per cent of their strength. People on the south coast of England saw the flames of the burning city under immense clouds of black smoke.

Very early in the morning of the 26th some motor-boats went into the harbour and took away about forty men from the end of the pier. At six that morning a boat took off from the north sea-wall ten men, who said that the Germans now controlled the harbour, meaning, probably, only the Carnot Basin. Another boat, going in, took off a load of French soldiers. After this a ship went in and took off 70 wounded, 3 civilians, 103 French and Belgian soldiers, and 50 British troops.

At 8 in the morning a flag of truce came from the enemy to our Brigadier, with a demand for instant surrender. This was refused. Almost at once the shelling recommenced, with a continual heavy bombing, which continued for hours. At midday some soldiers swam out to the *Conidaw,* and said that there were some wounded to go off. She put in and took away 165 wounded men. Our men were gradually overpowered. The French troops in the Citadel surrendered between 4.30 and 5 p.m. The 60th Rifles were surrounded about 6 p.m. and late that night the battle ended.

Soon after midnight on the 27th H.M.S. *Gulzar* came in, under Lieutenant C. V. Brammall, R.N. She tied up at the north Quai at the Gare Maritime. He landed his stretcher-parties, who were fired on by machine-guns. There were no signs of life. They called and hailed, but had no answers. Lieutenant Brammall withdrew his stretcher-parties and began to cast off for sea, thinking that no one was left alive there. As they cast off a solitary voice called "Oi".

Thinking that this was some German trap, the *Guhar*'s crew were very cautious. When they were satisfied that the hailer was English they drew in again and found three officers and 47 men; these they took off. They left Calais at 1.30 a.m.. They were the last men taken from Calais. Only one unwounded man came back from the Queen Victoria's Rifles.

Some days later a young officer, who had been captured in the town, escaped from the Germans, found a boat ("a dinghy") and rowed himself to Dover in her with a wounded arm and make-shift rowlocks.

Early in the morning of the 27th an English yacht sighted a raft bearing one French officer and two Belgian soldiers. These men were escaping from Calais. The raft was made of old wood and an old door. They had two tins of biscuits and six demijohns of wine. Also, carefully lashed on the raft, was an old bicycle. These men were saved.

Another small vessel picked up five other men on a raft. An officer of the 60th Rifles and two of the Brigade Staff Officers escaped from the Germans some days later and reached the mouth of the river Authie on 8th June. They had moved only at night and hid in the woods by day. Near the river-mouth they were joined by seven escaping French soldiers. Searching about, they found an old motor-boat which they patched up and managed to start. They were picked up near Folkestone on the 17th. These seem to have been the last to come home from Calais.

The Eighteenth Day, Monday, 27th May.

During the morning the enemy attacked the Wytschaete position in force, with his usual skill, at the two sensitive points, between the advanced battalions on the canal and their supporting brigades. Holding the battalion on our right, he attacked its supporting brigade and drove it backward. Attacking the supporting brigade on our left, he thrust that aside, and enfiladed the battalion it supported. Having thus isolated the advanced battalions he set about their destruction. The battalion on the right suffered very heavy losses. Its advanced companies and headquarters were cut off. "All the officers and most of the men of the two forward companies were never seen or heard of again." Without orders and heavily pressed the battalion came near to disaster. Some supports came up to help it: "We delivered a counter-attack with some cooks, batmen and pioneers." Meanwhile, the artillery did famous service. It had sent out a general order the night before: "Ammunition. Ammunition. Ammunition. Think of nothing else, steal it, loot it, send it up as you get it." Some had certainly been conveyed, and there it was to restore the battle. "From a farm behind the A Company's position some more reinforcements, pioneers, signallers and batmen came up, and we were ordered back to hold the line of road, and held these new positions against heavy shelling, mortar-fire and machine-gun."

Towards dusk the Guards and other support came up to counter-attack. By nightfall "the enemy seemed to have had enough for the day"; for some time he did not attack again, but kept shelling the positions. Presently, at one spot, the battle blazed up again, as a fresh British battalion came into the line. There was then heavy fighting at that part of the field. Elsewhere, it was an uneasy night for our men. "Nobody had any sleep that night, but by this time we were all accustomed to working without rest." In other parts of the line there was watchfulness. It was now a waning moon, dark till after midnight; no man there knew the country, a great many men were lost, and trying to find units or destination. Besides, all by this time knew how skilfully the enemy made use of this condition of darkness in a strange place to send out spies or agents who knew the country to prepare for his success upon the morrow. Nearly all our men were hungry, and there had been a great loss of officers.

One officer notes with feeling the difference made to some utterly dispirited men by the gift of "a hatful of hard-boiled eggs". After the gift they could face anything.

This very important battle kept our left throughout the 27th and made it reasonably secure. But this 27th was a critical and dangerous day for the B.E.F. The existence of the army was being threatened elsewhere, only twenty-miles to the west-south-west. Twenty disputed miles was now the width of the corridor by which we and our Allies might hope to reach the sea. Along forty miles of the southern side of this corridor there was an attacking enemy. On the north side there was a collapsing ally.

All along the British right flank (the southern side of the corridor), from La Bassée to Bergues, the enemy attacked, knowing well that his success there would be fatal to us. The story of his attacks and of our defences and counter-attacks may perhaps never be clearly known. No intenser fighting has ever been seen. Between La Bassée and Bethune the fighting on this day was often at the closest quarters, hand to hand; with intense and very accurate mortar and machine-gun fire. At Festubert the enemy attacked from south and north simultaneously, with light tanks and armoured cars, and presently followed this up by a great attack on the neighbouring town of Violaines, with about 300 tanks (light tanks leading, followed by medium size), about one medium to fifteen light. It was noted that the medium tanks fired incendiary shells, "very incendiary shells". Violaines was soon on fire throughout. The British commander notes: "Our anti-tank gun put twenty-one tanks out of action before it was itself destroyed". The tanks at last withdrew; the enemy infantry appeared "in perfect formation". Our artillery soon made them take cover; but they were in force and when our men had to withdraw they were surrounded and had to fight their way out.

There was an even stiffer battle about ten miles north-north-west from this, at the Forêt de Nieppe and the Lys Canal. Here the battle raged all day, under such a bombing from the air as no man had hitherto experienced. "Bombing reached peak. At one time no fewer than fifty-three machines counted." In addition to the bombs there was a great succession of attacks by tanks. One battalion alone was attacked by a hundred tanks. The brigade on its right was forced back through the forest by an overwhelming force; supported by

112

other tanks. Two famous battalions, one Welsh the other English, were in the heat of this battle, and at the end of it mustered only four junior lieutenants and eighty men between them.

The Divisional Commander kept in touch by telephone with his Brigadiers throughout this day. Once the enemy came in suddenly upon the telephone line. He addressed the Brigadier of one of the brigades by his Christian name, which he had heard the Divisional Commander using some moments before. His pronunciation showed him to be German; "he was told to go to blazes".

While this battle raged an attack was made four or five miles to the north-west at Hazebrouck, once a pleasant and prosperous town. This place, which was now a sort of outpost on our flank, was held by some companies of a good battalion. The attack began at 9.30 with about thirty tanks and a large German force advancing from St. Omer. "We were told we had better withdraw if we did not want to be wiped out. I said I had no orders to withdraw. There were thirty tanks and I took the artillery officer to see them. They were only about 1,400 yards away and massed closely, like vehicles at a race meeting. The artillery officer's mouth watered. 'If only I had some guns, but I am sorry, I cannot help; we have not got one'."

"At 12.45 the Germans bombarded us; the noise was terrific, but the effect negligible. There were literally masses of Germans 300 yards away. We opened vigorous fire with two Bren guns and the Germans ran."

However, they soon came on again, "although we could fire at them, we could not prevent them, and all round us fires had broken out from incendiary bombs. It was hopeless to get out of the building by daylight, all our lines of departure were covered by machine-guns. From the upper storey I got a very good view. At about 8 p.m. progress was seen to become slower; then four or five enemy bombers came over and bombed us. After the bombing it began to grow dusk. At about 9.30 all was quiet save for an occasional shot and the distant crack of the flames. I gave orders to withdraw. I pointed out that the column of fire we saw to the north was Dunquerque and had better make for the east of that. All was quiet. I led my men down the garden into the fields and thus the last position held by the battalion was vacated."

Meanwhile, three miles away, at Hondeghem, the enemy had

attacked in force at 7.30 a.m., "with an avalanche of tanks" which overwhelmed the two outlying guns, and then tried all morning to take the village. The two remaining British field-guns were so skilfully handled and served that the village was held till 4.15 p.m. against continual attack and under very heavy fire. At 4.15 p.m., as ammunition was almost gone and only one small party of reinforcements had arrived, and the whole little force was almost surrounded, it withdrew towards St. Sylvestre.

Unfortunately, St. Sylvestre was full of German tanks, "Germans appeared on all sides." However, the retreating force charged into them, "each man shouting, as ordered, at the top of his voice", and the Germans "broke in a panic". After this the party's troubles grew less. This detached battle is admirably described by Mr. Douglas Williams in the *Daily Telegraph* for Thursday, 19th September.

About three miles west-north-west from St. Sylvestre is the conspicuous, ancient and romantic hill-town of Cassel, from which a road runs almost due north to Bergues and Dunquerque. Midway between Cassel and Bergues is the little town of Wormhoudt.

All these places were of great importance to us. While we held them we could draw supplies from the Dunquerque beaches and retreat hither if we wished. If they fell into the enemy's hands, then our lot would be hard.

The 48th Division had been given the task of holding this part of the flank. It was now only two Brigades strong, since one of its Brigades was hotly engaged on the Comines Canal. Its other two Brigades took over the line from between Dunquerque and Bergues, through Wormhoudt to Cassel; as it was a line about eighteen miles long, and only two tired Brigades, without reinforcements, had to hold it, "the butter" as someone said, "had to be spread rather thin". One of these Brigades, the 145th, was put to the defence of Cassel.

Information had come in, from some captured enemy orders, that the next attack was to come upon Wormhoudt. It came, and continued to come throughout this day with tanks and infantry. There was thus thirty miles of determined battle all along one wall of the corridor by which we might hope to pass to safety. This was but a small part of the troubles besetting the British High Command. Though critically attacked on the right and left, with every reason to expect that the First French Army was being also attacked, he had

114

to arrange for the making of a defensive line about the beaches of Dunquerque, and try to discover what the plans of the French were.

It was difficult to communicate with anybody at this stage of the campaign. Wires were cut almost as soon as laid; messengers could not get through the jams on the roads, and all headquarters happened to be moving, like the armies. After trying in vain to find the French Commander-in-Chief, he went to Dunquerque, where in the evening he received the startling news that the King of the Belgians had sent to the German High Command that afternoon, to ask for an armistice from that midnight. It was a complication, that this important news was already necessarily known to the enemy. It meant that already the enemy would be taking advantage of it. Twenty miles of the northern wall of the corridor by which we could reach the sea was now so open to his forces that he could enter to cut us off without opposition.

Altogether the day had been 'not too bright for the Allied Cause'. There had been a similar day or two during the Great War, when things had seemed not sunny. Then our troops had burst into spontaneous song:

"We're up,
 We're up,
 We're up the blooming spout."

The reaction on this 27th May was much the same. Some have wondered at the slowness with which troops moved during this campaign. War is full of delays. In this war the roads were so crowded with people in flight that none but the ruthless could get by them. On this day an observer judged that five million refugees from the Netherlands, Belgium and Northern France, with animals, and every conceivable vehicle and burden, were clogging the roads leading to Paris by which troops might be moving to the help of France. In many places this stream of misery was being turned back by advancing troops. Sometimes, on being turned back, the unhappy people met the enemy and again turned back. The enemy did not always shoot or bomb them. Alive and wretched, they blocked the ways for the Allies; dead, they were of no further use to him.

It was on the morning of this melancholy day that Lieutenant-General Sir Ronald Adam began the preparation of the famous bridgehead, or perimeter, of Dunquerque, within which our army was to embark.

Nature and art had made ready to his hand a position of very considerable strength.

Between Dunquerque and Nieuport are beaches and dunes, shut in between the sea and a system of canals. The position is closed on the north-east by the canals and forts between Nieuport and Furnes. It is closed on the south-east by the canals and forts between Dunquerque and Bergues.

A big canal, linking Bergues with Furnes, makes a moat across its landward side. All the space enclosed thus between canals and the sea is much cut about with rhines and waterways.

It has one very great advantage. It is cut into two halves by the fortified French frontier in such a way that we could yield the eastern half to the enemy and yet hold a strong fortress in the western half. This fact was of much importance to us towards the end of the adventure.

The outer line of this bridgehead was now strengthened with what guns could be found. It was arranged that the 1st Corps of the B.E.F. should march into the west, the 2nd Corps of the B.E.F. into the east side of the enclosed space.

Dunquerque, being an important French city, was held to the end by what remained of the Seventh French Army. It was arranged that the First French Army should march into a part of the western side of the space, to that great suburb of Dunquerque known as Malo-les-Bains.

While these defences were being garrisoned the less-needed units of the B.E.F. were taking ship for England.

The Nineteenth Day, Tuesday, 28th May.

At 4 a.m. King Leopold surrendered, with almost all his army. The Germans gave orders that his army's weapons and warlike stores were not to be destroyed nor removed, but to be prize of war; they all fell into German hands.

During the 26th and 27th, the Belgians had suffered heavy losses; they were in a difficult position, short of supplies, wanting ammunition and disheartened by the ruin of their country. The effect of their surrender on the French people was very grave.

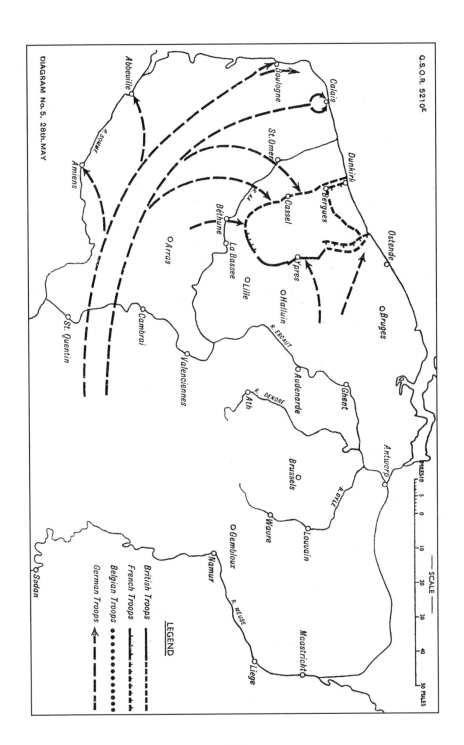

G.S.O.R. 5210E

DIAGRAM No. 5. 28th. MAY

LEGEND

British Troops
French Troops
Belgian Troops
German Troops

SCALE

5 0 10 20 30 40 50 MILES

The effects on the fortunes of the B.E.F. were likely to be swift and of the very gravest. It was necessary to guard the northern flank at once, and also to urge the French First Army into moving from its dangerous advanced position. One French General was against withdrawal, another said that his troops were too tired to withdraw. However, our orders were to withdraw, and to do that in safety the northern flank had to be guarded.

Meanwhile, the battle was continuing all round the B.E.F. On the Comines Canal there were repeated attacks, with many very clever infiltrations of parties of the enemy, and much most accurate mortar-fire. The enemy made several attempts near Warneton, but was held up by machine-gun fire. The fight was interrupted or made more difficult by violent rain and thunder in the afternoon; though attacks ceased, the battle continued with heavy fire all day long. In the evening our men received order to withdraw from the position through Poperinghe to the Yser.

The foresight of the British command had caused the preparation of a fortress to fall back upon. It was now our plan to pluck the army into this fortress through the walls of the corridor made by the two flanks.

The surrender of the Belgians had opened a door to the enemy right through one wall of this corridor. His motor and armoured columns had only to go thirty miles by fair roads or forty miles by excellent roads to come right on to the beaches in force and ruin our escape.

The line of the Yser River Canal from Nieuport Bains on the sea to Dixmude, about ten miles inland, was now of vital importance to us. There was a race between the enemy and ourselves for the prize. The destroyers off the coast could shell the excellent double road from Ostend. While they patrolled to watch for an enemy advance along the coast, some patrols of the mechanised Twelfth Lancers and a few officers of great determination hurried to Dixmude by road. They found some of the enemy, disguised as French and Belgian officers, already there.

Two officers, Second-Lieutenant E. C. Mann, D.S.O., of the 12th Lancers, and Lieutenant D. A. Smith, D.S.O., of the Royal Engineers, had been ordered to blow the bridges of the Yser Canal and to hinder any enemy advance there. "At the point of the revolver" they blew the bridges ten minutes before the enemy motor-cyclists came up, followed by a column of infantry in lorries. Lieutenant Mann was able to keep these enemies east of the Yser Canal for seven hours, during which time they tried to cross in all kinds of disguises, using every kind of ruse, now as refugees, with cattle, now as nuns or priests.

Few things in the war had such happy results for us as this holding of the Yser.

Many soldiers maintain that the enemy lost the race to the Yser because of the refugees on the roads. The weapon which they had contrived for our undoing turned against them and lost them the prize. But for that delay, they must have reached the Yser in strength before us and blocked our way to safety.

The march that night, of our troops towards the sea, stands out in the memories of many as one of peculiar horror and delay. It was dark till two in the morning (as dark as a summer night can be). It had rained very heavily, so that for the first time in the campaign the troops fought the real soldiers' enemy, mud. No troops could be spared for traffic direction; no lights could be shown, because of enemy bombers; many of the roads were under shell-fire; no drivers knew the roads nor the country, and all were weary from sleepless nights and continual fighting. They were hungry, too. One unit had received no regular rations for eleven days. One man wrote on the 17th that his battalion had had their first good sleep for a week. That sleep was the last good sleep they had had. On the 29th he wrote again: "It is impossible to get dates and times fixed; most of the men have completely forgotten the passage of time by now".

By this time, in some places, some of the First French Army were sharing the roads with us. Their transport drivers caused endless trouble by driving as was natural to them, on the right, instead of on the left as we did. In many places the narrow roads were blocked by cars two abreast, whose drivers had fallen asleep. Then the road would fill up behind the block, two or three abreast, horse-drawn carts and motors; other drivers fell asleep, and the jam would continue, till someone ran to the front of it and roused the sleepers.

One man, moving from the Ypres position, wrote: "Traffic this night took all possible first prizes, though we were spared French horse-drawn units. The night was as black as ink, Poperinghe a ghost-like town with ruined houses here and there; nobody to direct traffic except one over-wrought military policeman who knew nothing, anyway. A high velocity gun was firing intermittently on the town, but I doubt whether anyone cared. This particular nightmare had ceased to be a nightmare, by constant repetition."

One man, ordered to withdraw, found a shortage of more than thirty lorries in his transport. He went to report this to his divisional headquarters, and "became involved in a traffic jam which stretched two miles each way from the cross-roads. It became necessary to abandon the car, which was destroyed, and walk back five miles".

Many units, before setting out on this night march, destroyed all the kit and gear not utterly necessary to them before embarkation. Our lines were full of the melancholy fires of burning gear. Some of the severely wounded, who could not be moved without danger, had to be left in their hospitals, with a surgeon and five orderlies for every hundred patients —"who should stay was decided by drawing names out of a hat". The chaplains drew lots to decide which of them should stay with these wounded.

One man wrote: "On the 28th May this Battalion had been for nine days in operations; three days fighting at Oudenarde, three days severe fighting at Nieppe, and only one night of reasonable rest. For the last forty-eight hours meals had been intermittent; every man was soaked through. We moved on; transport blocked the road; the whole impression was one of chaos; often one had to turn right out of the road; often only one man could pass at a time.

"At Berthen the transport had been unmercifully bombed when caught in a jam (it is a tiny village with a road junction, just south of Poperinghe). Men had to climb over damaged vehicles to get through. In Poperinghe it was impossible to march as a formed body in the congestion of vehicles, horses, mules, bicycles and pedestrians."

One main cause of the trouble at Poperinghe turned out to be two French transport drivers who had left their lorries side by side in the road, completely blocking it, while they went off for a friendly hour in a cellar.

During all this day the troops entering the perimeter to embark made bonfires of stores, kit, and transport. The radiators were shot from cars, or their engines were forced to run till they seized. All secret documents were burned. Rumours, perhaps spread by enemy agents, declared that the enemy tanks had by this time cut off their retreat. It may well be that some few tanks did cross the line; but perhaps the real cause of the rumours was the jam of traffic. What, but enemy tanks could hold the traffic so? It was often a complete block, three abreast, lorries, cars, farm-carts, water-carts, wagons, limbers and every other vehicle, all jammed head to tail, while the bombers dived down and bombed and machine-gunned all the line. All who could, kept off the roads and went across country.

On the northern side of our corridor some of our troops had the satisfaction of watching the enemy put a barrage down on the positions they had left; "a complete attack was delivered against the deserted line".

On the southern and western sides of the corridor there was not much fun. The enemy was coming through in unexpected places. "In the later stages," a man wrote, "both the flanks and often the rear became fronts". A surgeon who thought himself six miles from the line was suddenly attacked by Germans, and had to jump into a ditch.

The enemy's great effort came on the right flank between Cassel and Bergues, for success there would have brought him triumph. He attacked hard throughout the day with tanks and infantry. The 144th Brigade held the northern end of the flank, the 145th held Cassel. If ever men died to save their fellows the men of those two brigades did.

Midway between Cassel and Wormhoudt, where this day's fighting was hardest, a German vehicle "ran into our road-block under the impression that the village was in German hands".

"Two runners arrived here with a message; it had taken them nearly five hours to come four miles (they had to cross the stream of traffic and the enemy attack). The enemy was continually attacking with short, intense mortar bombardments (the German mortars had an accurate range of about 3,000 yards), then an infantry attack accompanied by as many noise-producing fireworks as possible. Each time he seemed to get some success he was driven out by the bayonet."

As an observer wrote: "The enemy was always held on an adequately defended front and seemed to accept that fact, well knowing that he could get through elsewhere. His infantry, apart from patrols, did not work at night. They got adequate rest. We were fighting all day and frequently on the move all night, or, if not that, bringing up food, water, supplies and other matters. The enemy frequently lost opportunities of pressing home advantage after dark".

Sometimes on the ground the B.E.F. found adequate defence. It was when they looked up into the sky that they felt defenceless, for there they would see many enemy aeroplanes to every one of ours. Though our Air Force was fighting superbly, and doing wonders daily and nightly, its work was mainly bombing enemy concentrations and supplies behind the battle-fronts. Our men seldom had the comfort of seeing the enemy bombers attacked and brought down from over their heads. They were soon to see that sight frequently, and to draw much comfort from it.

What the enemy strength in the air was at this time may be judged from one fact, that at nine o'clock on this morning one soldier counted seventy-eight enemy aircraft over our lines; the vultures were thinking that they saw a carcass.

The Twentieth Day, Wednesday, 29th May.

The fight for Wormhoudt, Ledringhem and Cassel went on all through this day with varying fury. The enemy still hoped to cut us off there. The fight grew hotter in the afternoon. Near Ledringhem the enemy began to filter across the main road, so as to isolate the hill fortress of Cassel, where the 145th Brigade held out for the sake of the Army.

The enemy forces set free by the surrender of the Belgians were now coming in strength to attack the Yser positions on the east of the beaches. The evacuation from Dunquerque was in its fourth day; nearly fifty thousand men had gone.

There remained nearly six times that number to be lifted: the question arose, How many would be able to get away?

Boulogne was now occupied, Calais had fallen: all the guns, tanks and men used in the killing of those cities were now set free to wreck the B.E.F. They were all pressing on to the south-west of Dunquerque. Some enemy gunners had seized the French Fort Philippe with all its guns and shells at Gravelines. With these he was now shelling the city and the road to Dunquerque. Clouds of his bombers were blasting the area all day and all night. With such attacks delivered with such weight from the air, the east, the west and the south, what chance was there of escape for any of our men?

Men accustomed to weighing chances did not think that there was much chance.

There were, however, three strong helps coming to the rescue: the first was the Royal Navy; the second, the Merchant Service; and the third, the Royal Air Force.

These three were coming together, to hold the enemy and to pluck our Army from destruction. The Army, too, was full of fight and ready for anything.

As our Air Force had been forced to base upon England, our fighter-squadrons and all other machines of great petrol consumption and short range could only stay for a few minutes over French soil in each sortie. This gave another great advantage to the enemy, who already had an enormous advantage in number in every type of aircraft. Even so, the Royal Air Force took up the unequal challenge: with its two allies, it saved the army. The Army, as ever, surpassed itself when the luck was worst.

As the day began the enemy shelled the roads leading into the Dunquerque position. Only two of these roads were good; both, as it chanced, were in easy range, one towards each side of the position. Orders had been given to the B.E.F. to abandon all their vehicles outside the perimeter; but before these orders had been given many had entered. No such orders had been given to some of the French corps now moving in. The jams and confusions on the road impressed everybody. The troops coming in on this day were under orders for England, and nearly all were desperately tired. One man writes that the known strength of his Brigade, which had been fighting hard for nine days and nights, "was just about 100 men, mostly transport drivers". Frequently the weary lines of traffic were bombed; often drivers fell asleep at their wheels and stopped a long line, till someone ran along the line to rouse the sleeper and set the stream flowing again. One headquarters said "they hoped to clear the roads", a task which would have taken many men many days. It was never even attempted. The sight of the abandoned vehicles, some still with horses in the traces, some ditched, some crashed in the deep canal, the majority still blocking the three approaches, is one that will never be forgotten. One place was completely blocked by a string of lorries which had been bombed and burned. The Brigade collected Bren guns for the defence of the Canal (the southern defence of the perimeter) and then "had the first real sleep that many of them had had for many nights". Some of the scattered units of this Brigade were re-united on the beach, and reached England. It had left England with 90 officers and 2,500 other ranks; about 650 of these returned.

The vital points during these last days were the corners of the defensive line, at Bergues, on the southwest, and Furnes, on the east. At Furnes the enemy was now coming with a great many guns. All the approaches to it were under shell-fire and subject to the infiltration attacks at which the enemy was so clever. The mechanised cavalry fighting on this flank was much cut-up; one infantry battalion was reduced to about one company. Furnes itself had been shockingly bombed and shelled the day before, but when once in Furnes the troops found much good shelter in cellars (where enemy agents were sometimes found). Artillery found good positions on the French frontier line a couple of miles behind Furnes. At this place the hungry found a considerable amount of food in abandoned and damaged lorries. It was clear that the attack on Furnes would soon be pushed in great strength. Troops were moved to its defence.

In the centre, during that day, the Allied armies were moving into the perimeter. From an early hour the enemy shelled, dive-bombed and machine-gunned the moving troops. Again, as on the day before, the gravely wounded had to be left behind, sometimes with the devoted Belgian monks and Red Cross workers, sometimes with the doctors, orderlies and chaplains to whom the lots fell.

On the right the enemy's attacks called for strengthening of the lines. At one time there had been a gap in the line at Bergues; this was now well closed. Some battalions coming through the dunes to Bergues found a supply of rabbits which gave "a very savoury meal enjoyed by all". Another battalion, marching to Bergues from the beaches, found a garrison in the old fortress "of 17 officers and 1,000 men of many units, including half-trained troops, previously on the L. of C." These now received most sorely needed support. The battalion's companies took up their positions on the ramparts and in what cover the little old fort offered. The Canal de la Colme, the perimeter's main barrier, made a guard, of a sort, upon the north and the west of the walls. The one road bridge remaining over the canal led to the gate of the fort. Some small parties of English infantry held ground west of the walls; a French battalion lay beyond these, towards Dunquerque. The fort itself was of the late seventeenth century, with a moat adapted into a modern canal system. At the moment, the attack was not upon Bergues, but on the position at Cassel-Wormhoudt to the south of it, where fighting raged all day.

A message had been sent to the Commander of the force at Cassel, the 145th Brigade, giving him permission to withdraw, if he thought fit. The car in which the message went was ditched; it took twelve hours for it to get through. The Commander in Cassel was heavily engaged, and did not withdraw; he held on, and checked the enemy's advance. Up to 10 o'clock on the morning of this 29th, he had destroyed thirty-five enemy tanks at Cassel alone; he destroyed many more later. If these, with their supports, had got through at this point, and so on to Oost Cappel, it would have been a very serious matter.

Between Bergues and Cassel some companies of an English battalion had held a position all day upon the stream at Ledringhem against repeated attacks. At midnight, knowing that they were almost or wholly surrounded, the survivors began to withdraw, crawling along a hedge. "The whole place was lit by a burning wind-mill and burning houses. We followed the stream for some distance; then we found that our withdrawal had been discovered, for the village was lit with Very lights. We now cut across country by compass and came across Germans asleep in the grass. They were guards of a German battery. We took an officer and two men prisoner. We nearly had two pitched battles with two of our own parties whom we came across. We had lost these parties on leaving Ledringham. We came out on the road Wormhoudt to Cassel just as dawn was breaking (about 3.50 summer-time). We reached Rietveld. The village was occupied by Germans, who were asleep in the houses without a guard. The battalion proceeded through the village unmolested, had a short rest at Bambecque, and there took 'bus. As it took 'bus very heavy mortar fire began." The buses took them to the perimeter, they then marched to Bray Dunes, were rowed out to destroyers in small boats and were in England for the night.

When darkness fell the land was lit for miles by burning houses, dumps, cars, lorries and equipment. All that could not well be taken was burned. Oil-tanks blazed high. From time to time the fire in a line of smouldering cars would leap up and run along the road from car to car.

All through the night the shelling on the Furnes position increased.

The Twenty-First Day, Thursday, 30th May.

Furnes is a romantic little city fenced by a canal system. It was not grievously smashed in the last war; much of its ancient beauty remained to it. During the heroic defence of the Yser, in 1914–15, it was the headquarters of King Albert. The canal system, which makes a kind of moat to it, runs in a zig-zag about its southern and eastern walls towards Nieuport, where it joins the Yser.

Our troops were now holding Furnes and the canal. On their left, at Nieuport, the enemy was across the canal in places; on their right there was not yet much enemy pressure.

In the morning the enemy began a very heavy, accurate shelling of the city, and backed his shellfire by repeated bombing. So many shells burst close to General Headquarters that it was suspected that he had observers in the city directing the fire. A search was made, and an observation-post, with a civilian telephone, was found in the church-tower; the spy had gone. It was noticed that the churchtower (of St. Nicholas) was not once hit during the shelling. After a great shelling which caused few casualties, "owing to the excellence of the cellars", the enemy tried to cross the canal in small parties, using rubber boats. The boats burst when hit by bullets and the attack was driven off. The shelling began again and continued with growing power till late in the afternoon, when a great attempt was made, with "assault-boats", to cross the canal near the northern end of the town and create a bridge-head there. This attack was supported by very intense fire of every kind, "mortars, field-guns, 5.9 guns, machine-guns and light automatics. Under this fire some of them got across in a barge, and contrived to hold out on our side of the canal for some hours. The attack as a whole was beaten off by about 8 p.m., when the fire of the enemy slackened for the night." Many houses in Furnes were blazing. In the glare of the burning our troops attacked the platoon which had crossed to our side and drove them out of their position. At Bergues, at the other end of the perimeter, certain exhausted lines

126

of communication men were taken from the line and sent down to the beaches to be shipped for home. There was a good deal of fire towards the end of the day, but no pressed attack. The garrison found the day one of comparative comfort, after what they had endured in the ten preceding days.

At Cassel, after a long heroic defence of a vital point in the flank, the 145th Brigade withdrew what remained of its men. By this time it was cut off from its base; the enemy was between it and safety. "Very few of the officers and men of the 145th Brigade in Cassel reached the beaches; very few of them returned."

The enemy had crossed the road at Ledringhem and Wormhoudt, going east; he had come westwards from Dixmude; his two forces had met, and were now moving against the canal which made the boundary of the Dunquerque perimeter. The way to safety had been closed: but just too late. Almost all the Allies were now within the defence.

The Twenty-Second Day, Friday, 31st May.

The shelling of Furnes became heavier as the day advanced. At about 11 the enemy attacked the canal, under cover of mortar-fire. They got a pontoon bridge across and at once sent across men to spread fanwise right and left along the canal banks. In a counter-attack most of these men were driven back, "except in the centre".

In the evening, when the enemy fire died down, the garrison of Furnes began to withdraw; our line on the beach was being shortened, most of the army had been embarked. They marched on roads shelled continuously on to beaches being heavily bombed and machine-gunned. "There were occasional halts when officers and men lay down through sheer exhaustion. The Commanding Officer showed immense coolness and courage and was a real inspiration to all." On their left, at the hamlet of Moeres, there were explosions of ammunition and a general blaze. Some enemy shells had exploded some ammunition wagons; and the garrison was, moreover, blowing up machine-gun ammunition which could not be carried away. The bombing of the beaches this night was exceptionally severe.

The remains of the 2nd Corps were being withdrawn from the line for embarkation, leaving the 1st Corps with the French garrison of Dunquerque to hold the much-reduced perimeter, formed by Dunquerque and some floods on the right, by floods and the canal in the centre, and by the old French frontier defences on the left. While these things were being done the enemy made a vigorous effort to destroy the survivors.

At Bergues the enemy brought up a great array of mortars and opened fire with them. "These became a continual nuisance." Fires broke out in many places and bombing was almost unceasing. The headquarters were so accurately shelled that the presence of spies, directing the fire, was soon suspected. The spies were looked for, caught in the act of fire-direction, and shot. Enemy infantry gathered in groups as though to attack, but withdrew when fired on. Perhaps the place seemed not yet "ripe" for assault. The shelling and bombing went on all through the night; the streets were full of ruins and wounded men; many buildings were burning.

To the east of Bergues, along the line of the canal, the enemy prepared a strong attack from the little town of Hondschoote, where five roads led directly to the canal. A bend in the canal near this place offered him a prospect of success. He attacked at this point at dawn with very heavy fire from artillery, mortars and machine-guns, which continued for many hours.

The Twenty-Third Day, Saturday, 1st June.

At a little after midday the enemy crossed the Canal de la Colme to the west of Bergues, threatening to cut off the garrison's retreat. At 1.50 p.m. orders came to leave Bergues and hold a line two and a half miles north of it, near Coudekerque. As the advanced parties of the garrison withdrew they found that the enemy had crossed the canal to the east of the town and placed machine-guns in some farm buildings to check the withdrawal.

The withdrawal was upon a road with what were now considerable floods on each side of it. Something had to be done to check these machine-guns or the road would be impassable. Some men, therefore, put in an attack on the farm buildings by wading towards them, arm-pit deep in mud and water. Most of them were killed or wounded. The survivors reformed and made a second attack from another point which was not more successful. A third attack had this success, that it held the enemy's attention while the rest of the

128

garrison withdrew. Some of the men withdrawing "were up to the chin in water for over a mile".

All through this fight there was a great deal of low-flying, intensely heavy bombing and very accurate shell-fire.

The attack from Hondschoote came upon the canal line in force in the afternoon. The enemy crossed the water and drove back the defenders as far as a second canal, where they were held. Here, as they brought up their infantry, they came under clear observation from the Britsh battery positions near Moeres. These batteries, though they had few guns, had all the ammunition that was left. One battery officer notes: "The battery began to get most excellent shooting and were able to expend all remaining ammunition most profitably".

During the afternoon this battery heard the alarming news that the enemy had broken through on their right in the direction of Leffrinchoucke, thus cutting them off from Dunquerque. The news was false, the enemy was held, but it was clear that his reinforcements were coming to press the attack there.

The later withdrawals of the defenders at Bergues began at dusk and continued after dark, with much difficulty, owing to the numbers of wounded. These last companies moved independently under their company commanders to the Dunquerque beaches. "D Company of the First Battalion the Loyal Regiment remained at the Ypres Gate until 22.30, when they marched out as rear-guard." Somewhere on the road they found troop-carrying vehicles, in which they drove to the beaches.

At nightfall the French garrison of Dunquerque held the line from Fort Vallieres to Uxem and the survivors of our own First Corps held the rest of the now small perimeter. During the night the remainder of our Second Corps and of the First French Army took ship. It was "A still, close, dark night, lit dimly by a steady glow from Dunquerque and from a burning factory, and, intermittently, by the gun-flashes of French artillery firing lots of ammunition. French sentries kept challenging from the darkness, we were none too certain that we were on the right road, when suddenly we reached the beach and turned left towards the Mole. Into the final straight at last, but the finishing-post—the Mole—a most unpleasant-looking place seen from a mile or so. Apparently blazing like hell from end to end (this was really the oil-tanks behind it), crashes and bangs near the shore end, told us that it was being steadily bombed and shelled. 'Pick up the step there, chaps, left, right, left, right!' Suddenly a young staff officer was reached: 'Take your party down to the beach at once and get away in boats; lots are coming in.' Order obeyed with alacrity. Not so good when one paddled in, found many others paddling, no boats in and nobody knowing anything. Like a traffic jam, this muddle sorted itself out eventually, and before dawn most of the regiment were aboard some small craft or other; sixty or so were so unlucky as to be left on the beach at daylight. They were collected by their officers, taken to cellars for the day, and got on board the next night in first-class order."

More than sixty thousand men left the beaches that night.

The Twenty-Fourth Day, Sunday, 2nd June.

By dawn the B.E.F. had dwindled to the last rearguard of about three thousand men of different units with seven anti-aircraft guns, defending the harbour, and twelve anti-tank guns defending the eastward approaches to Dunquerque. The French garrison held the town and the Vallieres–Uxem line. Our men were scattered among the sands to lessen the casualties. They were bombed and shelled all day long: not attacked.

As the day ended the Germans drew nearer, drove back the French line and brought their guns along the beach. By midnight all the French and British soldiers under orders to sail had embarked; there remained only the French city garrison.

The Twenty Fifth Day, Monday, 3rd June.

Shortly after midnight the Commander of the First Corps with a naval officer went through the harbour and along the deserted beaches to make sure that the British were gone. Some stray German soldiers were already on the beaches and in the town; these were firing from time to time. The Commander writes: "Having satisfied myself that no British personnel remained on shore, I embarked".

The French garrison defended Dunquerque until nearly midnight, by which time most of their ammunition was gone, enemy tanks were in some of the streets, German machine-gunners were in the ruins, and advanced parties of bombers from both sides were exchanging grenades near the harbour.

Some of these small parties continued the battle until daybreak.

By that time Dunquerque had been a nine-days' wonder needing a story to itself.

DUNQUERQUE

DUNQUERQUE is an ancient sea-port, with a good depth of water, several docks, some building-slips, and the sea-mouths of three big canals. The city lies within a ring of old ramparts, all amply moated. Outside it, the coast stretches away to the east-north-east towards the Belgian frontier and Nieuport, the one eight, the other sixteen miles away.

This stretch of coast does not vary much in all those miles. Near the sea is an expanse of broad, shelving sand, in peace-time summers always thronged by multitudes of bathers. To shoreward there are digues, or sea-walls, of brick, and beyond them the sand-dune country, with rough sea-grass, a few poplars, a few windmills, and many drainage-channels. The sand-dunes change their shapes a good deal in heavy weather. To landward from the dunes there is a stretch about a mile broad where scrub and brush grow.

Within the last half century the stretch of beach has been much improved for the benefit of summer visitors. There are hotels, places of amusement, and a good coast road. Outside the walls of Dunquerque, to the east, is the seaside suburb of Malo les Bains, with a big Kursaal and Casino. Farther along the beach is a lesser pleasure place, Bray Dunes, also with a large Casino; and still farther to the east-north-east is the village of La Panne. This was at one time much visited by painters. In the Great War it became famous as the headquarters of King Albert of Belgium. In its churchyard there lies the body of a Belgian lady who was one of the victims of the *Lusitania*.

Though the coast may allure in the summer, it can be exceedingly dangerous both to seaman and landsman. In stormy winter weather one walking on the beach will be astounded by the violence of the surf and the distance to which its breakers stretch. As in parts of

Holland, he will feel at such times, that the sea is really above the land and may at any time engulf it.

The coast shelves gradually into the sea all along the beach. About three-quarters of a mile from low-water-mark there is the deep-water channel of the Rade de Dunquerque, with a steady depth of from forty to fifty feet, and a width of about half a mile. To seaward from this again are successions of sand-banks, some of them awash at low water, and all of them marine museums rich with the relics of ships.

"Oh, combien de marins, combien de capitaines." These shoals make a good protection to ships anchored in the Rade.

The tidal streams are often very strong here. Any northerly gale or fresh wind raises a dangerous sea upon the beaches and across the harbour entrance whenever it comes against a tide; an easterly gale will make an awkward sea at the harbour entrance. When a surf is running it breaks some distance from the shore, looks evil, and is much more evil than it looks.

Even in peace-time the deep-water approach to the port is not easy after dark. It is somewhat narrow for tides so strong. In war-time, when the navigation-beacons are extinguished, it may be very diffi-cult. In the present war, before the lifting of the B.E.F. began, certain ships had already laid their bones near the entrance to the harbour.

Piety in old time raised lofty towers to the churches near the coast here, to be guides to mariners. These towers still stand. They are impressive from the lowness of the land from which they spring, though perhaps modern man uses them more as artillery observa-tion posts than as sea-marks.

On the north side of the harbour of Dunquerque the ramparts are shut from the sea by a canal mouth fenced with a stone causeway about 900 yards long, known as the Promenade de la Digue. From the seaward end of this Promenade a strong wooden pier thrusts to the north-north-west into the sea; it is called the Jetée de l'Est: from its start from the Promenade it is about 1,400 yards long. From the beaches already described, from this long pier, and from the jetty to the west of the harbour the Allied Armies were lifted during the last week of the campaign.

Most of them marched along the east pier, or Mole, a "five-foot-wide wooden pathway", which remained a way until the end, in spite of all that the enemy could do. Commander J. C. Clouston,

R.N., who was its pier-master for a week (a record of great glory) was unhappily lost on 1st June. Some hundreds of men were killed and wounded on this pier; at least a quarter of a million reached safety by it.

Just one week after the first meeting held to consider the possibility of an evacuation from Dunquerque it became clear that the lifting must begin at once and continue with all possible speed.

Preparations of different kinds had been made during that week. A number of naval officers and seamen had been ordered for duty as beach-masters and beach parties; the Movement Control and Ministry of Shipping officials had also been busy. Troopships, hospital ships, supply ships and other craft had been detailed. All the enormous work of getting ready had been begun.

The Senior Naval Officer in charge of the Operation on shore at Dunquerque was Captain W. G. Tennant, C.B., M.V.O., R.N.

The docks at Dunquerque could now only be used by small vessels, as ships had been bombed and sunk within the Main Basin. In any case, the dock area was too hot from the burning warehouses and oil-fuel-tanks for men to use it much. Ships could still go alongside the wall in the Tidal Basin, but the approaches to it were made almost impassable by the intense heat and the continuous bombing. There remained only the East Pier, which had not been built for the berthing of ships, and might well give way under the strain of several thousand tons butting against it on a windy night. It had been built, in the main, as a groyne.

There were no piers along the nine or ten miles of beach, either to the east or west. Since embarkation from the pier alone would not suffice to lift the numbers in time, it was planned that the men should get into boats upon the beaches and be ferried to ships anchored in the channel off the shore. For many days a great deal of boat traffic had plied between ships and the beach. As the port proper could not be used, owing to the fires and bombing, our Army was largely supplied by such means; its bread, meat, drink and ammunition were landed there from boats, and still had to be landed.

Some foreign critics have written that it should have been easy for a maritime race, only forty miles from Dunquerque, to improvise a swift, effective service of ships and boats, and to lift the Army in a day.

War has a way of complicating even the simplest movement; and this was never a simple movement. Even in peace the business would not have been too easy. Tell even a skilled contractor that he is to send shipping forty-odd miles to ship over three hundred thousand men within a fortnight from one beach and one jetty, and bring them back the forty-odd miles; give him one week for preparation and another week for the deed, and how likely would he be to do it?

In peace the contractor would only have to telephone to hire shipping; he would be free to work without interruption, all would be easy, yet how many contractors in this world would be able to do it? Can you name one?

In war it is not easy to telephone to hire shipping. Every ship that can swim is in use in important national service; every boat is precious, and every life-boat round the coast is on duty. Every small coast-wise vessel is on duty that cannot be interrupted without danger. To gather a great number of ships in a hurry, to man them, equip them with instruments, charts, food,water, fuel,weapons and ammunition, is most difficult.

The forty miles of the journey were already subject to violent and continual attack from the air throughout, to danger from magnetic, floating and moored mines, to attack from submarines and motor-torpedo-boats. On the day on which the lifting of the Armies began, the enemy occupied the French forts near Calais and opened fire with medium artillery on all ships trying to use the usual entrance to the port. This made it necessary to find and use an alternative route. The Channel between England and France had been well and truly mined. Our own moored minefields made the alternative route rather more than eighty-six miles, or double the usual distance to be passed under the dangers mentioned above. As this was too long a journey, and certain to delay the embarkation dangerously, a third route had to be found. The third route made the journey about fifty-five miles. It could not be used at once, for it led across the minefields, which had to be swept clear, and over shoals which had to be sounded and buoyed, before ships could use it.

These were but some of the complications which war gave to the problem. The greatest complications were the war itself, with its ever-changing face and the fact that we were tied to Allies; each with urgent needs which were not necessarily ours. No man knew what the situation would be within the next few hours, and each of the three Allies wanted different things at once. The Belgians wanted us on their right flank; the French wanted us on their right flank; we wanted both of them to fall back quickly to end the very dangerous situation in which they stood; but both being on their native soil, wished to stay where they were. At this end of the campaign it was almost impossible to get news from these two armies, or even to learn where their headquarters lay. News or suggestions sent from either might be fifteen hours on the road, and come so late that both would be useless.

When the Operation Dynamo began it was thought that only a few thousand could be saved. The next day the situation was so much worse that we had to be prepared for a desperate scramble to pick up survivors from a great disaster. After this, as all the rear-guard actions so heroically fought had staved off the disaster, it was thought that the whole B.E.F. might be saved. But on the fifth day, when special effort was being made to lift the rearguard of the B.E.F., the whole arrangement was cancelled so that the French might be brought to England instead. The numbers given to the Officer-in-Command were "forty to fifty thousand". Later a hundred and fifty thousand or more were mentioned figures; in the end rather more than a hundred and twenty-three thousand Frenchmen were brought to England. This made the entire operation at least one-third bigger than anyone had thought possible, and this enormous increase in the work came suddenly upon those responsible after five frightful days, and at a time when death and destruction had thinned out the beach parties and smashed and sunk countless boats and many ships. The survivors were almost at the last gasp, the men were worn out, and nearly all the ships were in need of overhaul. It was upon these over-strained units that the extra work fell most heavily. It was this rising to the extra work right at the end which made the Operation Dynamo so magnificent a deed.

The pier at Dunquerque was under heavy attack continually; gaps were frequently bombed in it, and these had to be repaired with what could be found— ships' gangways, naval mess tables, etc. The beach had problems of its own. To begin with, the Army had not been trained for embarkation from an open beach, and some of it, when it reached the beach, was disorganised. Units were mixed up. Many of them had come into the perimeter after marching all night on roads jammed and blocked by transport. Many of them, officers

136

and men, were lost, and as a consequence there were units without officers and officers without authority. In any case, not many soldiers are used to boat-work, few have practised getting into boats from three or four feet of water when in uniform; nor is this feat easy, even in quiet water. It is a feat very difficult to do under heavy fire by men who have marched and fought with little sleep or food for seventeen days on end. The footing is firm sand, but whenever the tide ebbs and the wind sets on shore there is a swirl which makes boat-loading very hard.

Most of the embarkation had to be done by small ships, because only these could lie near the shore or enter the Channel at low water. All ships coming near to the coast were bombed. A bomb bursting near a small ship nearly always disarranged or broke some of her gear. In some cases the engines were lifted from their beds; gauges and fans were smashed, compasses dismantled or deranged, and feed-pipes broken. The losses in men were very great; in ships, severe, and in boats enormous. Those ordering this adventure in Dover had daily to replace men and repair or replace ships; for probably no ship returned from the beach undamaged. The minds which improvised this service had to be prepared for great losses which were certain to grow as the embarkation proceeded. Nothing but enormous heroic industry and utter self-sacrifice kept the ships steadily plying to and fro. The operation called into use 125 maintenance craft, in addition to all the carriers, for the maintenance alone was a nightmare. All the ships had to be refuelled. They were of many different types gathered anyhow; they needed many different kinds of coal, or oil or spare fittings. They had to be provisioned and watered, not only for their crews, but for the multitudes they had to bring. They needed an incredible number of rafts, ladders, brows, lifebuoys and grasslines. Often a ship's supplies of these things would be shot away in her first trip, and new ones had to be found on her return. Many thousands of the men brought were wounded. These had to have instant attention and special removal. Hundreds of the dead had to be landed for burial. New officers, crews, engine-room staffs and stokers had often to be found to take the places of the exhausted, the hurt and the dead. Many of the ships pressed into service had to be fitted with instruments; they had not even adjusted compasses. All had to be supplied somehow with duplicate drafts of the channels leading to Dunquerque harbour;

and as these channels varied with the passing of time and the sinking of ships at new points, these draughts and track charts had to be altered and marked.

It must be remembered that the ships and boats of all kinds only started to arrive after the order for evacuation had been given and the work had begun. The work, and the organisation of the work, had to proceed together. At one time there were as many as a hundred and fifty craft anchored outside Dover Harbour, while another fifty waited in the Downs for orders and supplies.

Knowing some of the difficulties, I should say that the Operation was the greatest thing this nation has ever done.

Troopships sailed for Dunquerque in the afternoon of Sunday, the 26th May. It had been arranged that two ships should call every four hours at the jetty, while drifters should stay off the beaches to receive men ferried out by motor-launches. The Operation, which received the name of Dynamo, began at 6.57 that evening. The first ship of the Operation returned to Dover with troops at 10.30 that night; her load was of 1,312 base units and lines of communication men.

Dunquerque had been frequently and heavily bombed daily and nightly for some weeks; it was on fire in many places, and blazing to heaven from its oil-tanks. For the next week bombs must have fallen on or near it every five minutes. It was reckoned that in the Great War it received in all some 7,600 bombs; this record (though considerable) was easily passed now, for the enemy sent over immense flights, in the almost certainty of success.

Wherever his bombers flew they had a perfect target beneath them, columns crowded on roads, shipping crowded in a channel, masses of men upon a beach. During the week there were three hundred and fifty thousand men shut in within a narrow compass with all their possessions; any bomb-dropping anywhere inside the perimeter was certain to be destructive. These bombers and their masters exulted at the sight. For the first time a great German encircling movement was to be helped to complete triumph by mastery in the air. Sedan had been a victory; this was to be an annihilation.

Monday, 27th May.

At an early hour the enemy began his effort to annihilate. Nelson said long ago: "Only numbers can annihilate": the enemy had the numbers. He had us penned in within a ditch and the sea; death was round three sides of us and above us: and no doubt death came down upon us. What our men faced in those days is hard to imagine.

The enemy had long boasted (and had paid others to boast) of the overwhelming might of his air force. He had the might: no doubt of that: he had the target of his dreams, and the prize of a century. No other place in the war offered such a prize. By putting all his bombers on to the beaches and the harbour entrance all day and all night long for one week of time he might do something which would fill all the headlines of the Press of the world.

The people of this island have never cared much for the headlines of the Press: in their dumb way they have cared a good deal for what will look well in a ballad. Now, when the enemy bombers came over in their numbers to annihilate, the little groups of our fighters took them on. Our fighters were few and could not stay over the beaches for more than fifteen to twenty minutes at a time: in countless cases they returned to England on their last gallon of petrol: but while they were over the beaches each little group would tackle fifty. The usual enemy formation was of ten to twenty bombers, with protecting fighters above them "arranged in steps", sometimes fifty strong. One British pilot, on this 27th, reports meeting a formation of between forty and fifty enemy fighters; he attacked them single-handed and made them split up. Another attacked six German bombers single-handed, and having fired off all his ammunition on them had to break off the battle; as he did so he ran into fifteen enemy fighters. He went into cloud to avoid these, having now no means of fighting; and came out of the cloud on to another twelve with the first fifteen still close behind him. He promptly made for more cloud, but, before he could reach it, was attacked by yet another twelve coming from the west. The skilful enemy often fled to draw our fighters into traps. "The enemy led us into very concentrated A.A. fire, which was very accurate up to a height of two miles and more. Tracer and flaming bullets which left a pink trail were observed to stream past very close. We carried out aerobatics to evade the A.A. fire, which was intense and had a very demoralising effect upon us." Still, at the end of the day one of these "very demoralised" men attacked forty enemy planes single-handed over the beach. Always in these days our fighters were so greatly outnumbered that they were hardly noticed by the men on the beaches whom they helped to save.

139

One of the drawbacks of fighting over the beaches was that if the aviator had to take to his parachute and drift slowly down, he became a target for many thousands of Belgian, British and French soldiers who imagined him to be a "parachutist". One man so floating down reckoned that twenty thousand rounds were fired at him as he came; all missing. Another says: "As I floated down I gave the Belgian soldiers and peasants five minutes' simple pleasure by acting as a target. Fortunately, their skill was not greater than their intelligence, and I was rescued by the B.E.F. One enthusiast even took a last shot at me while I was talking to the officer".

This 27th was a bad day for the lifting of the troops. Calais had fallen the night before. The enemy lost no moment in seizing and equipping the good gun positions on the high ground at Les Hemmes and in manning the guns in the French fort of Grand Philippe. He opened fire with these upon the ships trying to enter Dunquerque by the usual passage from the west. His fire was so heavy and so accurate from these points that five transports had to turn back, a sixth was badly hit, and a seventh, while being shelled, was bombed from the air and sunk. This showed those in command that the short western route to the harbour could now only be used in darkness. There was nothing for it but to send the transports right round the French and English minefields so as to enter Dunquerque from the east by what is known as the Zuydecoote Pass. This route made the round voyage 172 miles instead of 80. Unfortunately the mine-sweepers had not finished the sweeping of this route; still, the need was so great that it had to be used. At the same time minesweepers were at once sent to sweep a shorter channel across the shoals and mine-fields between the beaches and England. This shorter route, when ready, made the round voyage 108 miles, but the sweeping and buoying took some time, and was not completed till the 28th. The enemy well knew what was being done and sent bombers on to both routes to sink the sweepers.

In other ways the day was disastrous. Two strings of valuable boats were lost. They were being towed to the beaches by tugs before dawn; in the darkness the tows were run down and the boats scattered. This was especially unfortunate, because there was a great shortage of boats suitable for beach work. There were thirty small ships off the beaches receiving men, but so few boats that they had to use their own. The cry of the day was for boats of the whaler type (sharp at both ends) and for skilled boatmen. The naval beach-parties were of the greatest possible help. Most of them passed most of this day up to their waists in water helping soldiers into boats. All the time the enemy bombers were bombing and machine-gunning the workers.

The results of the day were not encouraging. Five troopships took from the harbour 3,952 men between them. The drifters, using ship's boats, lifted something like another 2,000 men from the beaches. A day's total of 6,000 men, when there were more than 300,000 to lift, was such a poor score that many people began to think that the operation would be a failure. The weather prospects were not too good. There was a heavy-weather system in the Atlantic: it seemed to be moving north: but if it moved even a little to the east, it might raise such a sea that the boats would be unable to ply upon the beaches.

Tuesday, 28th May.

We were lucky because the storm passed to the north along the west coast of Ireland; only the extreme fringe of its secondary was felt in the Channel. However, even the fringe was bad enough. A surf got up on the beaches and swamped a good many boats, besides being most exhausting to the boats' crews. Other boats were lost by the lack of skilled boatmen. Soldiers coming off in boats often let them drift away as soon as they had reached a ship. The problem of embarkation was made more complex by the fact that on this day the beaches had to be used for the landing of water. By this time there was an acute shortage of drinking water in Dunquerque and on all the beaches; not less than 150,000 men were thirsty there. At least 50,000 more men, the entire Third Corps, were expected at the La Panne beach, and water had to be found. The ships contrived to land a good deal in tanks and petrol-tins.

All through the day our fighter squadrons continued their efforts to check the enemy bombing. There are several accounts of flights of three British pilots attacking formations of fifty enemy aircraft. One flight of three attacked a formation of seventy-two. One man mentions coming into forty-five bombers guarded by fighters engaged in dive-bombing the ships and craft just off the shore. Frequently our airmen met formations of thirty bombers attended by twenty fighters. In the afternoon, when the enemy made a very great and terrible bombing attack, one man counted ninety-five enemy aeroplanes over the beaches at once.

By this time there was so much smoke from the burnings over Dunquerque and the beaches that it was difficult for the enemy to see what was going on. Still, we lost on this day two trawlers by mines, two drifters and a troopship by bombs, and one minesweeper sunk in collision.

During the day some skoots approaching the harbour entrance were hailed by a skoot coming out. The hailer said that Dunquerque had now fallen into German hands and that the evacuation was over. This report was not due to enemy guile, but to a misunderstanding of what some soldier had said.

Wednesday, 29th May.

The troopships used the inner side of the East Pier throughout the day. A naval officer has described what he saw on these occasions. The first things seen by him, as his ship went along the eastern pass, were what seemed to be vast black shadows on the pale sands. In front of him, as he went in, was the blackness of smoke with tongues of flame shooting into it. On the sands were these blacknesses; he could not think what they were.

As it grew lighter he saw that the blacknesses were enormous formations of men standing, waiting. He saw them thus whenever he entered the pass, coming or going. They did not seem to change; they did not seem to sit, nor to lie down; they stood, with the patience of their race, waiting their turn. He was present throughout the evacuation. The thing which impressed him most in all the week was this thing which had so impressed him so deeply at the first, the patient presence of these thousands, silently waiting, among the racket of bombing, shelling and machine-gunning, the roar of planes, guns, rifles and fires.

In the day-time there was both work and pleasure on the beaches. Water, food and ammunition were landed and carried up; the sick and wounded were carried down; meals were cooked and eaten; the troops under orders to embark formed and marched to their embarkation points. One or two who were there mention football on the beaches, "trick-riding on military bicycles" and "pleasure-paddling". All through the days of the evacuation the troops came flooding into the perimeter, Belgians in some number, the First French Army, and more and more of the B.E.F. All agreed that the bombing, though atrocious, continual and very trying, was not very deadly. One man said: "If ever I have to be bombed again, give me a sandy beach, for the bomb sinks in and hurts very few when it bursts."

Three witnesses agree that the first days of the evacuation were the worst, partly because the machine had not begun to work smoothly, either from the lack of equipment or from the failure of troops and boats to arrive when each needed the other; and partly because the first men lifted were not disciplined men; they were camp-keepers, store-keepers, drivers, and lines of communication men. "The men became better and better as the evacuation continued. After the first day the men were nearly all well behaved, patient and orderly, On the last two days they were superb."

"It was wonderful to see them at the end, almost dead-beat, but clean shaven and some of them singing,"

"The French soldiers took longer to embark than ours; they never liked to embark save as complete units." "They were extraordinarily thoughtful; often we could not get them to share our rations, as they thought that we were short of food."

A naval officer, who was there, says that throughout the evacuation an elderly British soldier stood at the seaward end of the pier, quite unmoved by anything that was happening. In peace-time such a figure would have stood selling evening papers; this man seemed to do nothing save collect rifles.

At the shoreward end of the Fast Pier was a deep and very good cellar, where many men sheltered and many wounded were treated. Throughout the evacuation an English woman lived in this cellar. It was said that she was a London woman whose family lived in Dunquerque. She was always cheery and helpful, looking after the wounded, and making tea for the weary. It is hoped by many that she reached England safely.

The weather during this 29th May was bad. One of the nuisances of the day was the density of the smoke about the harbour entrance. As the surf was running on most of the beach the harbour had to be used for the chief embarkations; so much black smoke from the burnings was driving down that the harbour entrance was often very difficult to find. Men in the harbour could not see what lay in the roads. One naval officer reported that there were no destroyers in the roads; as a matter of fact, there were then ten present. The men ordered for embarkation marched along the long wooden gangway of the East Pier to the ships. The smoke screened them from the sight of the enemy bombers, but many bombs were dropped at random on to them. The enemy was now shelling the harbour heavily, though not very accurately; he could not observe the bursting of his shells. Two of our destroyers were torpedoed in the early hours of the morning while bound for Dover laden with troops. The loss of lives was very heavy. Our ships opened fire on a vessel to the south-west; she blew up with a bright flash. She was thought to have been the enemy motor-torpedo-boat which sank our ships. During the afternoon the embarkation was going fairly well, at the rate of about two thousand men an hour. The smoke was now a little clearer; a shift of wind was setting it inland. We had ten ships inside the pier, loading men, and four other ships waiting to come in. As this made a target which the enemy observers could not fail to see, a great force of bombers was sent against it. For two and a half hours, from about four o'clock, it rained bombs on the harbour entrance; and grievous harm was done.

Three of the ships at the pier got clear, much damaged; three were set on fire; one of these burning ships, the *Grenade,* seemed about to sink in the fairway; no doubt she would have sunk but for prompt action: a trawler towed her luckily clear in time. The *Verity,* coming out of the harbour entrance, struck on a sunken drifter and nearly added her bones to the pile. An old British destroyer, H.M.S. *Sabre,* built by Stephen in 1918, among the most famous of the many ships famous for their share in this week, on emerging from the harbour found some men struggling in the water. "Having no boats, for all her boats were with the first-lieutenant lifting men from the beach, she manœuvred alongside each man in turn and picked them up. While doing this she was repeatedly dive-bombed."

There seems to be little doubt that this bombing was the worst during the operation. It caused ruin on the pier and a chaos of burning and wreckage among the ships. Lieutenant Robert Bill, D.S.O., R.N., by a swift, sailor-like decision, saved the harbour entrance from being blocked by wrecks..

At 6 that evening the ship *King Orry* coming in found the harbour occupied only by burning and sinking ships; there were no soldiers on the pier and no ships moving. She stayed there till after midnight, at first under heavy bombing. Some hospital ships were very heavily bombed at 6.30. At 7 a report was passed that the harbour entrance was blocked by wreck. Luckily this rumour was false. By 7 the fury of the bombing was over; the harbour was not much bombed after dark.

The surf had made boat-work impossible at certain places on the beach, and very difficult and exhausting elsewhere. Some had been done.

The boats of H.M.S. *Jaguar* took off troops from Bray beach "for fourteen or sixteen hours continuously, the boats' crews going without food, wet through and subject to frequent bombing attacks". Four hundred men were brought off from Bray to the s.s. *Bideford*. While these were coming aboard a bomb struck the ship abaft all, and blew forty feet off her stern. Surgeon-Lieutenant John Jordan, M.B., R.N., though his sick-berth attendant was seriously wounded, stayed in the sick-bay and dealt with some fifty casualties, many of them horribly mutilated or dangerously wounded, and performed several major operations. He was helped by George William Crowther of the 6th Field Ambulance, who had been embarked from Bray beach and volunteered to help the surgeon. When the other unwounded troops had been transferred to another ship he said he would stay by the *Bideford*, "knowing her to be aground and unlikely to reach England". She did reach England. The *Locust* gave her a thirty-hour tow; she reached Dover on the 31st. H.M.S. *Calcutta* had her boats in the surf all day on this day as on the day before. H.M.S. *Vanquisher* made a record of two round trips during the day.

All who were on the beaches learned this day that the enemy had drawn a good deal nearer on both sides; he had captured Mardyck Fort to the west and occupied Nieuport to the east. Rumours came in from enemy sources that he meant to employ "four air divisions against us" this day, and that he meant to attack English aerodromes and eastern seaports that afternoon. This may have been a crude attempt to keep our Air Force in England while he overwhelmed us on the beach. Certainly our air observers saw that he was bringing up his armies. Eighty tanks and large columns of lorries were seen approaching from the north and the east. The surrender of the

Belgian Army had released against us an enemy column three miles long which was coming down upon us from Belgium. One sailor passing along the coast that night picked up three soldiers from a raft: He saw fires burning all along the Belgian coast, four great fires burning in Dunquerque, and a line of ships stretching twenty or thirty miles along the coast, bringing troops away. Here and there great black patches of oil on the water marked the graves of ships or aeroplanes. It was reckoned that about 38,000 troops were lifted on this day. Considering the badness of the surf and the bombing, this was not a bad total. The losses had been great. Three destroyers and four troopships had been sunk, eight other ships sunk or badly damaged, and eleven severely shaken by bombs and needing instant repair. The glass was rising; weather reports from out at sea showed that there was a chance of calm water on the morrow.

Thursday, 30th May.

The weather was now improving; the light wind was almost easterly and the surf gone. The engineers could now start to build piers into the sea from the beaches. They built these with army lorries and whatever deckings, scantlings and gratings could be found. These piers were of much use to the soldiers going off in boats. The boats could lie alongside them and the men no longer had to wade out waist-deep to get aboard them. The naval beach-parties, who had passed three days in the water helping men into boats, now had a slight, very slight, improvement in their lot. Some of the small paddle-steamers and other craft engaged in the lifting tried to come alongside these piers. This was not a success. The pier-ends were not sufficiently firm to stand the strain. Invention was being tried along the beaches. Grass-line was sent for; various devices were tried for heaving off strings of boats together on messengers of grass-line. Some masters tried the device of butting small ships head-on into the beach, and then drawing up to the sterns of these ships, so that soldiers might use the lesser ships as gangways to the bigger. These devices sometimes worked and sometimes failed, according to the local conditions and the skill of the men. Our seamen, indeed, the seamen of all races, are ready, resourceful men. The condition of the B.E.F., with its left flank laid open by the Belgian surrender, called for all the invention and resource within the race.

146

The wrecks from the day before had made the harbour entrance difficult; still, it could be used by one ship at a time. Early in the morning a Store-ship came alongside the East Pier with necessary provisions. The boxes of food blocked the pier for a time. One well-known Channel steamer, the *Princess Maud,* on this day noted the number of wrecks and the narrowness of the swept channel by which ships came and went; it varied from 250 to 490 feet; this did not give much room for error in a crowded way, subject to violent currents, in which all sorts of accidents to steering gear might happen at any instant. One such accident came to her. "A salvo of shells knocked a hole in the engine-room a yard square." The men got mattresses into the hole and "prevented a great deal of water from entering". She had to turn back for repairs, which took some days. On her way back she noted "wreckage, rafts and numerous craft of all kinds" plying on the route. By this time the nation was awake to the glory of the effort, and Dynamo was in the triumph of its swing. Nearly eight hundred small craft had been called to the work, with an unreckoned number of ships' boats. These were now plying to and fro along the dangerous and glorious narrow alley, under bombings and shellfire from an over-armed enemy. The change in the weather raised hope in every heart. What the embarkation meant on this day can be judged from a few quotations from diaries for this day.

"We proceeded to walk into the sea to embark in two boats at 10.30 p.m. After rowing for three hours, having tried to board two warships which moved away just before we could hail them, we boarded a minesweeper at 2 a.m. At 3 a.m. she ran aground and we transferred to another mine-sweeper."

"Men were marshalled into groups of fifty by means of a megaphone and a cornet, each group being under an officer. About 8,000 or 9,000 men of the Division were passed through."

At one time during this day 4,000 troops were embarked within the hour. As the sea was calm much greater loads could be carried in each ship. One destroyer, following the precedent set at Boulogne, took 1,400 men in one trip; it made her a bit of a handful, but all went well. The yacht *Conidaw,* which had so distinguished herself at Calais, a ship eighty feet long, over-all, made a trip with eighty soldiers in addition to her crew. Some of the best beach-work was done by some Dutch skoots and Belgian mail-packet ships with

English naval crews. This was the fifth consecutive day of the adventure. The seamen reckoned it the last of the worst days. By this time some of the destroyers' crews were nearly exhausted, for they had hardly slept since the operation began. Some spare hands were distributed among them. They had not been asked for. The naval ratings had but one thought, to get to Dover with a load, and then get back to Dunquerque for another. In all, on this day, 45,955 men were lifted. Five ships were damaged, and the *King Orry*, a sixth ship, badly hit, foundered on getting out of the harbour. The cook of the *Bystander* (Mr. J. H. Elton) was on the deck of his ship at the time. As the *King Orry* sank he saw at once that many of the troops in her were much too exhausted to swim. Many of the men embarked on this day had suffered a great deal in the ten days before they embarked. Mr. Elton dived overboard with a rope to save them and remained in the water for thirty minutes, during which he rescued twenty-five officers and men. On coming aboard again he went to his galley (which was equipped with cooking utensils for seven) and in the next half-hour supplied ninety-seven soldiers with hot tea and food.

Haze and low-flying cloud made the enemy bombing much less effective on this day. Another thing which contributed a great deal to the comparatively small list of losses was the extraordinary, resolute valour of our fighting Air Force, which on this day surpassed itself by wrecking seventy-six enemy 'planes with a loss of five of its own. One patrol shot down twenty-one; one squadron of twelve shot down nineteen. One seaman noted in his diary for this day: "Things getting worse, but everybody happy."

Perhaps it was on this day (I have been unable to fix the date) that Mr. B. A. Smith, in the motor-boat *Constant Nymph,* with a crew of two, who had never before been to sea, ferried off about 800 men to two skoots. After this he collected boats that were drifting round, and towed other boatloads off amid bombing and shelling.

Friday, 31st May.

During the night the enemy laid a great many magnetic mines by air along all the approaches to the harbour. These were added anxieties, but not very fatal. He had brought up more batteries and was now shelling the beaches more heavily from both sides. All through the night the transports sailed. When morning dawned the beaches were nearly clear, though more troops were on the road and pressing into the area. The troops of the First French Army were due to begin to embark this morning.

Just after sunrise the easterly wind freshened. At once the surf began to run upon the beaches and boats capsized. Early in the day the jetty at Bray, newly-built of lorries, was broken by the surf and shell-fire combined. The enemy had by this time come further west along the beaches. He had now guns in battery, with which he could shell all the Zuydecoote Pass. A good many light craft were sunk. By this time the boat service on the beaches had much improved. There were more whalers, and a very large number of small power-boats, which did much better than the miscellaneous ship's boats in use hitherto. One ship was sunk during this day and two damaged.

While the surf was running Captain W. A. Young, commanding the *Levenwood*, of 800 tons, was asked to put the nose of his ship into the sand and to keep steaming slowly ahead so as to avoid going broadside on in the rising tide. In this position he got out a "messenger" or revolving hawser to the shore, and sent boats in and out by it. He was bombed all the time while in this position, but none of the bombs fell nearer to him than 100 yards. Mr. Moodey, one of his firemen, kept going over the side and swimming to the wading soldiers. He encouraged those who could swim to strike out to the boats. He swam back with the too weary men who might have collapsed; he actually carried or supported all those who could not swim. He did this for three hours in a heavy swell and surf.

One very great benefit received during this day was a ship-load of collapsible boats and pontoons.

This day's surf, having displaced, soon broke up the derelict lorries which had been used in the building of the pier. The broken relics washed about in the breakers and were a great danger to the boats. Other sources of very great danger were drifting clothing and grassline. Thousands of soldiers' greatcoats were floating. These fouled the screws of the motor-boats, which were then frequently made unmanageable and swamped in the surf. The surf was "Less dangerous during the afternoon", as two seamen note.

During the afternoon, H.M.S. *Skipjack*, when filled with troops and towing a motor-boat, was attacked by dive-bombers. She shot down three aircraft, but five bombs from one plane struck her. She turned over and sank. The survivors were picked up by a neighbouring destroyer and reached Dover. One man writing of this day says: "Ammunition was going up like fireworks. I waded out to my armpits and scrambled aboard a boat. Two others jumped out of the boat and completely swamped her. We spent about two hours trying to re-float her, but the seas were too strong. I decided to look for a change of clothes and searched the beach, where I soon picked up some short pants and socks. On returning, I found my party gone. I picked up some biscuits on the beach and presently, when I boarded the destroyer, I had an enormous feast of bread, bully-beef and tea."

Another man writes: "We reached the East Jetty at 11 p.m. On one place there had been a direct hit on the Mole. The gap had been patched with boards. A final halt was made 200 yards from the end, which was altogether about a mile long. Most of the men laid down on the jetty and went to sleep in spite of the cold. A German bomber flew over us at one o'clock, dropping bombs. The battalion just behind us was heavily shelled and machine-gunned and suffered severe casualties. Two ships had already been sunk at the end of the jetty. It was apparently impossible to embark till the tide rose.

"At five o'clock a destroyer drew alongside. It was daylight, but luckily there was a mist. We were conducted below and all were very soon asleep."

All through the day there were the usual heavy bombings by the enemy. They were frequently sending over companies of bombers twenty-five or thirty strong, supported by fighters. During all this day our great effort in the air was against the German forces advancing from the east and west. In the evening our bombers dropped over sixty tons of bombs on Germans approaching from the east. One squadron dropped eight tons of bombs on Germans advancing towards Furnes and another company dropped ten tons of bombs on assemblies of tanks moving towards Cassel. Unfortunately, the troops inside the Dunquerque lines could not have the comfort of watching these attacks.

One shipmaster, writing of this day, says: "We soon had about 200 soldiers on board. The stewards were employed getting food for men who had had but one meal in the last three days. The doctor, who was Jewish, on being told that there was pork in the stew, said, 'I do not care if there are dead dogs in it, I'm going to have my share'.

The homeward route was a wonderful sight. Hundreds of small craft of every description, making towards Dunquerque. The German bombers were busy dropping their loads all over the place. There were more than seventy enemy planes overhead dropping their bombs all round on us, like hail-stones, but our luck held good. We escaped undamaged. The gunner put in some great work with his gun and hit three enemy planes, two of which came down. I was just coming along Folkestone pier at 8.30, when a violent explosion occurred. Another lucky escape. A mine had gone off behind us. We had brought home 504 troops, seventy of them French."

It was a most successful day for those lifting troops. 59,797 were brought to England.

Among the remarkable feats of the day must be mentioned that of Able-Seaman S. Palmer, in the thirty-foot motor-yacht *Maid Errant*. Putting into the beach in the surf, she was rushed and swamped by French soldiers. She was then washed ashore. He refloated her. He had no crew, save one stoker, but he gathered a British N.C.O. and eight soldiers and with these put off for England. The engine was not working well and at last broke down. He then broke up the wood fittings of the yacht, into paddles, and induced the eight soldiers to paddle. He reached Dover safely and set forth again the next day for another trip, but was stopped, as it was felt that the *Maid Errant* was too slow for the work.

Saturday, 1st June.

On this day the enemy made his most determined effort to ruin the lifting. The Master Mariner had written on the 30th that things were getting worse; they now became much worse. From midnight until five in the morning, the shelling increased to such a pitch that of the two hospital ships sent in for wounded, only one was able to go in to bring them off. The other lay off the harbour entrance for four hours, but could not get in. Four troopships tried to get in, and failed. One entered at dawn, loaded up, and was returning, when she was heavily bombed. Our troops were out of La Panne, but enemy shells fell there.

At five o'clock the enemy let loose a monstrous air attack all over the area. It lasted for four hours, with successions of aeroplanes thirty to forty strong; one Master Mariner made the note, "Over

100 bombs on ships near here since 5.30". We were making, or hoping to make a very great effort, to lift the rest of the armies on this day; the enemy was bent on stopping us. We tried all the routes. All were now under very heavy shell-fire. It was reckoned that the enemy had at least three batteries of six-inch guns near Gravelines, besides the heavy coastal guns in Fort Grand Philippe. The French ships, using this approach, were much shelled; several were sunk. At six that evening the signal was sent from the harbour, "Things are getting very hot for ships". It was decided that the harbour could no longer be used during daylight. A naval officer had the heart-breaking task of telling the men waiting on the jetty that they would have to go back and wait for night to fall. During the darkness a great effort was to be made; small ships were to take men from the beaches to the east; about a hundred small French ships were to take French soldiers from the beach at Malo; we were to have twenty-four ships, as well as power-boats, at and inside the jetty; the French were to send ships to the Quai of the new outer harbour. This meant, that between 9 p.m. and 3 a.m. something like two hundred and fifty small vessels would be at sea in a narrow channel without beacons or navigating lights, with all the officers overstrained, all the ships overloaded, all the crews overworked, on a night of last quarter-moon, as black as a summer night can be, in waters with considerable current, certain to be sown with mines, all of them under shell-fire, and likely to be bombed. The burning buildings in the ruins of Dunquerque were the only lights that guided those mariners. The Admiral from Dover controlled the traffic; a Dutch naval officer and Dutch crew, under Commander Maund led the ships in.

The lifting on this day was a record; we took away 61,998 men in spite of the appalling fire. Our loss in troopships, destroyers and mine-sweepers sunk and damaged was very heavy.

By this time many soldiers had learned something of the manage-ment of boats in sea-ways; they were of much help during this day. All day long upon the beaches the boats were plying under continual dive-bombing and machine-gunning. Many boats were sunk or capsized by these attacks. In those parts of the beach where there was surf (and there was always surf somewhere) a capsizing caused confusion, from men being unable to swim, or so wounded that they could not swim. The dive-bombers flew over the water machine-gunning all that they saw. Men on the beaches replied with Bren guns.

One ship leaving the pier with a thousand men on board was attacked by eighteen dive-bombers. The bombs killed forty and wounded two hundred and forty of those on deck. She had three doctors on board, "but it was very difficult to treat the wounded owing to the crowd. An oil-pipe was burst in the engine-room; the ship had to be towed, but presently could proceed under her own steam". Our Air Force again did heroic deeds all day. One squadron at about noon on this day attacked a formation of between fifty and sixty enemy fighters and drove them all inland; another squadron engaged a formation of eighty.

Among the countless gallant deeds of those days the work of the two fine motor-boats *Marasole* and *Pauleteer* must be mentioned. These were in charge of Mr. D. T. Banks, who began in the *Marasole* with a crew of two ordinary seamen, a Bren gun, a Lewis gun, "and a compass which he did not know how to use". He completed seven or eight trips, and brought back more than four hundred men. When the *Marasole* was sunk he continued with the *Pauleteer* under frequent machine-gun fire. At times he took a run ashore in Dunquerque, then burning fiercely and under intense bombing.

More than one observer mentions the scene upon the crowded routes. "All sorts of craft were coming round the buoy, all fully loaded with troops. A batch of about twenty Belgian fishing-boats bore down, the leader asking us the way to England. I sung out the course, and told him to follow the other traffic and he would be all right."

The log of H.M.S. *Sandown*, Commander K. M. Greig, D.S.O., R.N., for this day may be quoted:

02.35. Anchored off the N. Goodwin Sands in response S.O.S. from *Golden Gift* ashore high and dry with 250 troops on board. Took off troops in motor-boat in five trips and returned to Ramsgate to disembark troops.

11.00. Proceeded to Bray and anchored there 14.30. Shelling from Nieuport batteries. Embarked 900 British troops. Heavy air attacks and 6in. shelling throughout afternoon, necessitating shifting billet on two occasions.

23.30. Weighed. Two magnetic mines dropped by plane close to.

5.00. Disembarked troops.

Remarks. Embarking troops was carried out under difficult circumstances owing to heavy shelling, air attacks and swell running, which made boat-work very arduous. The spirit of the officers and men was excellent. Ratings volunteered from the stokehold for any duties required.

On this day seventy-eight enemy aeroplanes were destroyed over the Dunquerque beaches.

Sunday, 2nd June.

Very early in the morning some of the men from Bergues marched to the end of the Mole, which they reached just before daylight. There they found a fully-laden ship casting off for home. The naval officers told the men that they had better go back to the beaches before daylight, to be safe from air attack. "The return to the beach was very slow; the Mole was long, all ranks were exhausted and hungry, and there were two lines of troops, the French on the left, the British on the right, and when our men moved back to the beaches, the French were still moving forward towards the sea." (They were being lifted by the French.) The disappointed men marched back to the beach, and there some of them launched a boat from a derelict oil-tanker and got aboard a French drifter, which anchored in the Road, and endured many bombing attacks, till she was fully loaded. The rest of the battalion dug themselves into a canal bank, till night, when they came away in a destroyer.

Another unit, which had fired its last rounds, destroyed its guns and wrecked its wireless sets, was also turned back from the Mole end, and passed a dreary day of bombing and shelling at Malo. "Malo was packed with thousands of deserted vehicles. The Mole (the East Pier) is about 1¾ miles long, and stands twenty feet above the water: Accurate salvoes of 5.9's continued every ten minutes, but they only shelled one end at a time. There were always plenty of gaps in the Mole." These troops got away a little later than those mentioned above.

This day, being Sunday, a Chaplain held Holy Communion on the beach and dunes. His congregation was scattered five times by low-diving bombers, but reassembled each time till the service ended.

As an anticyclone was now centred over England, the Channel was calm, with a good deal of haze. What light breaths blew tended to carry the smoke of the burning city over the harbour entrance and its approaches; it was very difficult for mariners to see their way in.

There had been much fighting in the perimeter during the last few days; at Furnes and at Bergues many men had been wounded. It was felt that possibly some of these grievously hurt men might be permitted to leave without molestation. The Geneva Convention, which provides for the safe passage of hospital ships carrying none but wounded soldiers, had been accepted by Germany. An appeal was therefore clearly wirelessed at 10.30 this morning. "Wounded situation acute and Hospital Ships to enter during day. Geneva Convention will be honourably observed and it is felt that the enemy will refrain from attacking."

Hospital carriers had already suffered a good deal during the lifting, though showing the illuminated Red Cross and flying Red Cross flags. Their logs say "The vessel was heavily bombed; eight hands reported suffering from shell-shock. The attacks on these hospital ships were deliberate."

"On one occasion, at 8.15 on the 31st, she had seven separate air attacks. A magnetic mine fell so close that we had to reverse to avoid. Twenty minutes later another mine blew up less than a hundred yards ahead. It partially lifted the ship out of the water. Another dropped ahead only four feet away, but did not explode. We were continually worried by aircraft."

After the wireless message had been issued, two hospital ships, the *Paris* and the *Worthing,* sailed to bring off the wounded. The *Worthing* was attacked by twelve bombers and forced to return. At 7.15 p.m. the *Paris* reported that she was bombed, badly hit and in danger. Tugs were sent to her, but she was sinking, and went down after midnight. The bombing which wrecked her took place in full daylight, somewhere about 7 p.m. Men in a ship just astern of her at the time "saw the German aeroplanes machine-gunning the boats which contained nurses and medical personnel." A Master Mariner who went to the rescue says: "We had a job of work with the hospital ships. *Paris* survivors had been bombed and machine-gunned. Rendered assistance to ninety-five survivors, including five nurses who were seriously wounded." He adds that: "Most of the

155

ships which went into Dunquerque were hit more or less badly. In most of them their compasses were disorganized by explosions, and they were difficult to steer and often leaky."

As these last atrocities made it impossible for us to take certain of the more grievously wounded men, it was decided that chaplains, doctors and orderlies should draw lots, as on past occasions, for the honour of staying to look after them. The lots were drawn; the wounded were left in charge of those to whom the lots fell. So far as I can learn they have not yet been exchanged.

An observer writes: "The sky was absolutely black from burning oil; the air was full of black, oily smuts; all the sea was edged and coated with smut; the men were either black with oil-smut or splashed with grey mud flung up by shells between the tide-marks. What struck me most was the number of French and Belgian dogs which had attached themselves to the armies. It was sad to see them trying to come on board the ships. Hundreds of them were shot." A good many were brought to England, and their quarantine money subscribed for by the troops.

At about 4.45 that afternoon, three of the R.A.F. fighters sighted three enemy formations near Dunquerque. Each of these formations was about a dozen bombers, cruising around in great circles from which, from time to time, single bombers swooped down to bomb and shoot at the trawlers and boats.

The three R.A.F. fighters split up, to attack.

One went straight at a bomber just climbing from an attack and shot it down into the sea. He then went at a second bomber and shot that down, too. He then went at a third and put it down out of control. On rising from this third flight, the airman found the enemy all gone, except for one bomber making for the shelter of clouds.

The second of the three R.A.F. men attacked and chased two of the enemy bombers over Dunquerque. One of them plunged out of control into the smoke of the burning city. The airman then turned to attack about twenty bombers still circling over the approaches; he at once attacked them and put one down, damaged.

The third R.A.F. man meanwhile attacked a group of three enemy bombers. His battle was taken over by three other British fighters; he rejoined his two original companions, and with them drove off two bombers which attacked them.

Soon afterwards, the three saw below them two big ship's boats, full of troops, not under way. Two of our fighters went to find help for these boats, while the third cruised above them, to guard them. Eight enemy planes attacked him; he went for all the eight, and drove the formation back over Dunquerque.

These three fighters had shot down two enemies certainly; they judged that two others never flew again, and three others were damaged, one, very severely. Not one of the three fighters had been hit. The two fighters found help for the boats. Two tugs came up to look after them, and brought them into safety. Fifty-six enemy aeroplanes were shot down over the beaches on this day.

Soon after this, the great lifting of the day began. We sent in sixty vessels with many boats. The French sent in ten ships and 120 fishing boats. A great effort was needed, for the line was now very short; the enemy was pressing on the French garrison towards Uxem, and sending guns along the beach to shell the pier.

While going back with a load of troops that evening, the Master of the *Royal Daffodil* saw German aircraft machine-gunning the *Paris* hospital ship's boats, containing nurses and hospital attendants. His own ship was attacked by six enemy aircraft soon afterwards. Five salvoes missed him; a bomb from the sixth went through three of her decks into the engine-room, and then out through the starboard side before bursting; the engines stopped; the enemy 'planes machine-gunned the ship and set her on fire. She was by this time listing heavily to starboard. Her Master, Captain G. Johnson, very promptly shifted all her gear to port, lowered all her port boats into the sea and let them fill with water. The weight thus brought to port tilted the hole clear of the sea. While some put out the fire, her two engineers, Mr. J. Coulthard and Mr. W. Evans, took all the beds they could find and plugged the hole with them. When the leak was thus checked, Mr. Evans stood up to the neck in water, holding open a bilge-valve, while Mr. Coulthard kept the pumps going. In this way they reached Ramsgate, "the engines going very slowly, as the Diesel had three parts of water to one of oil." She landed her seamen safely, probably about 1,500 in this trip. In all this ship brought away 8,000 men.

On board her at the time was "the soldier W. C. E. Smith, R.A.M.C., who did excellent work, attending to the sick and wounded." He won from the captain such a tribute as few men can ever hope to win, "I have never seen a soldier at sea play the part of a sailor so well. He behaved in a most gallant manner the whole time. . . . When there is no doctor on board it makes it doubly difficult".

One of the wounded tells me that he lay on a stretcher on the sand for two days close to Dunquerque, "in a cloud of grey smoke", and heard the shells going over all day and all night long. He was taken off by a destroyer on this night.

During all this last period, our men were holding the line outside the eastern side of Dunquerque, helped by fire from destroyers in the Road. We were taking very great numbers of French troops, for nearly all our men had gone. The last men in the line were called out of it that night; at 11.30 p.m. the Senior Naval Officer reported "B.E.F. evacuated."

In all, 31,427 men had been brought away that day, with a loss of one hospital ship and two trawlers sunk; and one hospital ship, one cruiser, one destroyer and one trawler severely damaged. Of course, few ships escaped without receiving damage of some kind. At eight on this evening one of our transports sighted a sailing barge in need of help. Several sailing barges had been used in the service, having good capacity and small draught. This one now contained only soldiers, who had somehow sailed her over almost to the Goodwins without any sailors. What had become of her crew? Possibly, she had been towed to Dunquerque without a crew; she was now towed home to safety.

In the account of this day something must be written of the loss of Commander Clouston, R.N., who had for six anxious days been "doing noble service on the jetty at Dunquerque."

On Saturday night he returned to Dover to report upon the situation and to receive final orders for the great lifting of troops planned for Sunday night. He left Dover on this day in a motor-launch with a naval officer and some seamen. A second motor-launch came with them. On their way they were attacked by enemy aircraft, who put his motor-launch out of action and left her in a sinking condition. Commander Clouston waved to the men in the second launch to get away before they were sunk. With the naval officer, the only survivor of his Company, he then left his wrecked launch to try to swim to a boat seen a couple of miles away. Becoming weary long before he could reach this boat he turned to swim back to the water-logged launch, and was never seen again.

His companion, after swimming for two or three hours, reached the boat he had sighted and with great difficulty got on board her. She proved to be a ship's deserted cutter. In this he drifted for some time till picked up by a French trawler which had lost her way in the Channel. He undertook to navigate this trawler back to Ramsgate, and did so. Later he reported at Dover dressed in clothes borrowed from a French sailor.

Commander Clouston had been of the utmost service in helping the escape of nearly two hundred thousand men under frightful conditions of strain and danger. It was a grief to many that he did not live to see the lifting brought to an end.

Monday, 3rd June.

Early in this day, the R.A.F. sent large patrols over the Dunquerque area. They found no enemy targets, aircraft or troop columns, in the district. They went on to Bergues and Gravelines to bomb the batteries which had been so very grievous to us. The bombing was heavy; no gun fired from Bergues for a considerable time afterwards.

We urged the French to make every effort to end the lifting during this night. The anticyclone, which had given a blessed calm during the critical days of the lifting, was now slowly edging to the north. The wind was north-easterly, making an unpleasant and dangerous jobble at the harbour entrance. The fine weather haze thickened into fog, so that several ships had to anchor in the Road.

The fog and smoke were a hindrance to us and to the enemy. His airmen and guns made great efforts to see what was going on by firing star-shells and flares over the dangerous approach just east of the harbour entrance, where the traffic and the wrecks were thickest. Besides the old known wrecks on the charts, there were now at least twelve others, three to the west, nine to the east, seven of them in the fairway; more wrecks lay in the harbour. Ships had to hang about at the entrance in the jobble of the tide, trying to keep clear of wrecks and traffic till they were signalled to enter. Even inside the entrance, in the darkness, ships were frequently banging into each other or into the jetty as one left and another took a berth.

H.M.S. *Express* and H.M.S. *Shikari* were the last ships to leave, H.M.S. *Express* at 3.18, H.M.S. *Shikari* at 3.40. The enemy tried to bomb H.M.S. *Shikari;* luckily, the haze made the aim poor. These two ships carried between them about one thousand soldiers and the British pier parties. The only troops now remaining in Dunquerque were some non-combatants of the garrison, and the few units still holding the fortress for the French. After the last ships had left, some motor-boats, containing the last of the British naval ratings, went through the harbour to make sure that all had been brought away. For some days past, demolition parties had been blowing up harbour equipment which might serve the enemy; this work was now done, as far as possible. Some of the enemy had now crept right into Dunquerque; some of them fired from time to time, with their automatics. The naval officers were struck by the silence which had fallen after the racket and roar of the last week; now there came only a shot or two now and then. As the last boat left the port an officer in her was shocked by the mess and disorder. This had been a great and busy seaport, full of order and industry; now it was a filthy, black, smouldering heap of ruins, with dead ships in the harbour and at both sides of the entrance, dead men floating in the sea, and washing up to the beach; the wrecks of aeroplanes lying about, and an inconceivable litter of broken transport, packing-cases, old clothes and smashed weapons. He had a horror of leaving all this mess not cleared up and made tidy. He had been in charge of the beach since the operations began. Neither he nor any of the naval ratings under him had had any rest to speak of for eight or nine days. As he went out he thought of the thing which had so impressed him on one of his visits at dawn, of the great black formations of men patiently waiting on the sands. Through his work and that of our seamen all those patient men had been taken away.

An Admiralty message ended the Operation Dynamo at 2.23 p.m.

Though the lifting was finished, some useful cruising was done later, to pick up stragglers. The R.A.F. and a number of motor-boats cruised over the Channel, and helped to find and save men wrecked in a transport and in a barge.

Some French soldiers were lifted from Dunquerque harbour during the next midnight, by French and English ships, the last ship (the *Princess Maud*) leaving at 1.50 on the 4th. As she left, a shell fell in the berth she had occupied a moment before.

It is said that the white flag was hoisted on the ruins of Dunquerque at nine o'clock that morning.

On the 5th, a motor-boat picked up thirty-three French soldiers and two naval ratings. A few more drifting soldiers were picked up by patrols during the next few days. About 1,100 came to England in small parties in Belgian and French trawlers. Many strange escapes were made. A French lieutenant arrived at Dunquerque with nineteen men; they embarked in a boat and got aboard a wrecked passenger-ship lying in two fathoms of water. Here they camped without food or drink for a week, making fires of wood. Four of them built a raft, went off in her, and were seen no more. Seven others died of thirst and exposure. In the evening of 12th June, the survivors were seen by a British aeroplane, who reported them to the patrols; a motor-boat went out at once and brought off the lieutenant and eight men, with their rifles and kit. These must have been among the last to be saved.

The numbers lifted and brought to England from Dunquerque alone during the operation were:

British	186,587
French	123,095
Brought by hospital ships, etc. ..	6,981
	316,663

THE lifting was a wonderful improvisation by the seamen of this people. The landsmen played their parts, too, from the Staff Officer, who spent twelve hours of one day up to the waist in water, helping to push off boats, to the oarsmen, who volunteered to bear a hand.

The Masters of ninety-one merchant ships, of fifty-seven passenger- and store-ships, and of thirty-four tugs were thanked for their share in the work. One authority says that 665 small craft were employed off the beaches, as well as a great number of ships' boats. The Port of London alone sent thirty-four motor life-boats and 881 ships' boats. "These small craft lifted more than 100,000 men." "No boat ceased work as long as troops were in sight on shore." "As the boats were sunk, the crews went elsewhere, into other boats, and carried on." Of the civilians working there, four were killed and two wounded. Of the merchant seamen engaged, 125 were killed and eighty-one wounded. Six English and seven French destroyers were sunk. 171 English ships were repaired during the operation. Many of the repairs were of a serious kind, as in the case of the *Royal Daffodil,* yet the work was done so quickly that the ship returned to the task. "About 1,000 charts were issued; 600 of these had routes laid off on them for those who had no equipment."

"Many of the boats had not even a compass and no navigational instruments other than a lead pencil, and if they once lost contact with their convoy their chances of getting there in the strong currents was very slight. . . . Some boats got to Calais, instead of Dunquerque, where they received a rousing reception from the Boche."

"Many of the boats were from the Thames Estuary. They had never before left the Estuary, and only one of their crews had been further than Ramsgate, but the conduct of the crews of all these boats was exemplary. One 35-foot motor-launch ferried off 600 men to transports and carried 420 direct to England."

Such an assemblage of destroyers, drifters, dan-layers, Dutch trawlers and skoots, mine-sweepers, ferry-boats, tugs, river and pleasure steamers has never before plied the Channel. The London tug *Nicholas Drew* went there towing twelve life-boats; the famous London fire-boat, the *Massey Shaw,* went with a fire service crew, brought off sixty men and carried them to England. Later, with a naval crew, she tendered-off some hundreds, then carried home forty-six and returned to the beach for more. At the home ports 670 troop trains carried the soldiers away. Volunteer war workers provided mobile canteens to all these trains, to give food, drink, sweets and cigarettes to all, and to send off telegrams for those who wished.

What the service could be may be judged by the following. On the 1st of June, one ship, crossing to Dunquerque, was six times attacked by dive-bombers. While alongside at the jetty, she was attacked again. On leaving, full of men, she was attacked twelve times, and so much damaged that she had to anchor for ninety minutes while she repaired her steam-pipes. During these ninety minutes she was attacked continuously. She then returned home. Yet under these conditions many ships made several trips. The old destroyer, H.M.S. *Sabre,* made nine trips; H.M.S. *Malcolm* made eight trips; the *Royal Daffodil* made seven, and was turned back from an eighth; H.M.S. *Codrington* made seven trips. The *Leda* and the *Medway Queen* seven each; H.M.S. *Shikari* and H.M.S. *Vanquisher,* seven each; H.M.S. *Vanquisher* and many others making two on one day. Many ships made six trips. H.M.S. *Princess Elizabeth* worked without stopping for four days and nights. I have mentioned the endurance of the thirty naval officers and 320 naval ratings employed ashore as beach-parties; how living a strength is generosity. Most of the destroyers' crews worked to the very brink of exhaustion; in some ships of the Channel ferry services the crews went on till they dropped.

Hundreds of little vessels from half the coast of England deserve to have their names in the Navy henceforward.

The enemy had proclaimed our complete encirclement and destruction; no doubt he had expected to achieve both aims. He did not do these things, because he could not. He came up against inundations and defences which checked his tanks; he had not enough infantry and guns to overcome our defence. He came up against our Air Force, which attacked him with complete in-difference to the numbers he sent against it. He came up against our Navy, which is a body not easily checked by danger or difficulty. Lastly, he came up against the spirit of this Nation, which, when roused, will do great things. The Nation rose to the lifting of the Armies as to no other event in recent times. It was an inspiration to all, to feel that will to save, running through the land. The event was as swift as Life; no possible preparation could be made; the thing fell suddenly, and had to be met on the instant. Instantly, in reply to the threat, came the will to help from the whole marine population of these islands. Word passed that the armies were shipwrecked on the sands; at once the lifeboats put out, and kept plying as long as there was anyone to lift.

Our Army did not save Belgium; that is a little matter compared with the great matter, that it tried to. In the effort, it lost thirty thousand men, all its transport, all its guns, all its illusions; it never lost its heart.

The Nation said to those men, in effect: "Hold on; we will get you away." They held on, and we got them away.

It is hard to think of those dark formations on the sand, waiting in the rain of death, without the knowledge, that Hope and Help are stronger things than death. Hope and Help came together in their power into the minds of thousands of simple men, who went out in the Operation Dynamo and plucked them from ruin.

THIS account of the campaign in Belgium and France is necessarily very brief and imperfect. Many of those who took part in the operations are on service in distant parts or prisoners of war. Many of the records of the operations have been lost by fire or water; many have not yet been sorted or cannot yet be made public. As time passes, it may be possible to add to this record, to remove some of its defects and to clear up much that is now perplexing.

I wish to thank all those officers of the Army who have helped me with information, maps, papers and suggestions.

Among these let me thank especially Colonel the Lord Bridgeman, M.C., Colonel Neville, M.C., Lieutenant-Colonel K. Strong and Colonel Hooper, Major G. H. Bolster, Major J. M. Hailey, Major J. R. Kennedy, Major M. Reid, M.C., Major B. Reynolds and Major A. F. Sinclair.

I would also thank Mr. G. W. Lambert, of the War Office, and Mr. H. A. Cordery, of the War Records Office, for making simple a task which without them would have been very difficult to do.

I am deeply indebted to Air Commodore Peake, of the Air Ministry, for the welcome and help given to my plans by him. I thank Mr. J. C. Nerney, the Librarian of the Air Ministry, for looking out for me so much that had to be studied.

I thank Captain Brooking, R.N., for a delightful and busy afternoon at the Admiralty, making a first acquaintance with the Operation Dynamo.

I thank the Deputy-Keeper, the Secretary and the Assistant Keepers of the Public Record Office, for much courteous help.

It is difficult for me to express my thanks to Vice-Admiral Sir Bertram Ramsay, K.C.B., M.V.O., for his never-failing help during the last month, when already sufficiently occupied by bombardment from the enemy and the possibilities of invasion. I am grateful for all the information he has given me and for the track-chart supplied by him and reproduced in this book.*

I am deeply indebted to Captain F. W. Bush, D.S.O., D.S.C., R.N., for his most moving account of things seen at Dunquerque. I thank

* The track chart does not appear in the 1941 proof.

165

Commander K. M. Greig, D.S.O., R.N., Lieutenant R. Bill, D.S.O., R.N., Lieutenant-Commander R. C. Wardrop, R.N. Lieutenant-Commander P. F. Cammiade, R.N., and Sub-Lieutenant J. Mason, R.N., for clearing up doubtful points and helping me to understand what happened off the French coast in that critical time.

I thank Lieutenant H. Powell, R.N.V.R., for his clear photograph of the Dynamo Room, where this great Operation was planned and kept going.

I thank Miss Marjorie Bell for her help with the official photographs used as illustrations.*

I warmly thank Mr. B. E. Bellamy and Mr. W. G. Hynard, of the Ministry of Shipping, for making my work there so easy and so pleasant.

I thank Mr. N. K. Johnson, D.Sc., the Director of the Meteorological Office, for letting me consult the weather charts for the vital days of the campaign. Perhaps the weather which gave the enemy so much advantage did at last help to save us from ruin.

I thank Professor Charles Webster, Mrs. Baker and Miss Beard, of the Royal Institute of International Affairs, for help with countless press-cuttings from the newspapers of the world.

I thank Miss E. M. Roads, O.B.E., for her help in the manuscript's last stages.

I thank Mrs. Roxbee, Miss Jenkins, Miss Somerville, Miss Taylor and Miss Walton, for long, patient and often laborious copying, sometimes under difficult conditions, and for the accuracy, neatness and quickness of all their work.

I must not end this list without thanking some who have been particularly helpful in other ways; among these let me name Mrs. Hamilton of the Ministry of Information and Mr. A. D. Divine, until lately of the Ministry of Information, and Sir Stephen Gaselee, D.Litt., C.B.E., F.S.A., of the Foreign Office.

JOHN MASEFIELD

---

* A plate section was obviously envisaged. Indeed a page listing headed 'Maps and Illustrations' is present in the 1941 proof but alas the illustrations are not present.

In the black Maytime when we faced the worst
And saw the punishment that Nature deals
To Nations ranking fat unwisdom first,
And the iron Judge rejected all appeals,
Then, when no other human light appeared,
And men surmised the bitter truth untold,
That we were lost, and that disaster neared,
To rank us with the empires lost of old,
Then, comfort came, for suddenly we knew
A forethought and a courage and a skill
Descending out of Heaven from a few
To smite aside the certainty of ill,
And Hope returned, and those we longed to save
Were given Life and lifted from the grave.

When someone somewhere bids the bombing cease,
And ships unharassed ply at Life's demands,
And friends again greet friends in foreign lands,
And sad survivors call the ruin peace,

Then, peace will be but ruin, unless Thought
Of how the peace was purchased be in mind,
Of how, to buy it, men are lying blind
Under the sea in ruined wreckage caught;

Thinking of them, and those who rode the air,
Or shogged the Flanders plain in Belgium's aid,
Or stood at Cassel with the grand Brigade,
Peace may be filled with beauty everywhere,

If, with each purchased breath, we vow to give
To Earth the joy they never lived to live.

Not any drums nor bugles with Last Post
For these men dead in intellect's despite:
Think not of war as pageant but as blight
Famine and blasting to the pilgrim ghost.

So, for the brave men fallen for man's crime
The young men beautiful all unfulfilled,
The broken and the mangled and the killed.
For whom no Spring can come in cuckoo-time

Let there be beauty spilt like holy seed
Not any mock of custom or parade
But hope atoning for the ruin made
And shame alike for deed and want of deed.

O smiling, sun-burned youth who rode the sky
Like to the sparrow-hawk or summer swift,
And watched your shadow flitting on the drift
Far underneath you as you hurried by,

Six months ago to-day you put off bird
To gleam as ion in a nation's will
To save the ruined friends and then lie still,
Spring never to be touched by summer's word.

Often unseen by those you helped to save
You rode the air above that foreign dune
And died like the unutterably brave
That so your friends might see the English June

Haply, in some sharp instant in mid-sky
When you at the bird's summit, took the lunge
Of the foe's bitterness that made you die,
And the bright bird declined into her plunge,

You, from the Heaven saw, in English chalk
White, about Dover, some familiar track,
That feet of yours would never again walk
Since you were killed and never coming back,

Yet knew, that your young life, as price paid over
Let thousands live to tread that track to Dover.

Let a people reading stories full of anguish
Showing mighty Nations humbled by a blindness,
By a want of wisdom, scorn or hate of knowledge,
Insolence in office,
Emptiness of mind or indolence in office,
Cringing to the false one and the true denying,
Boasting of the self gift while the un-self scorning;
Anything save labour,
Let them recollect that bright Imagination
Smiting with her sun-flash will, like hosts of angels,
Shine so that her hundreds pluck the many millions
Even from disaster.

Ah, when the spirit knows the dewy dawn, the peacetime, Friend
will meet fellow coming in their thousands to the stage,
There will be quiet there in expectation of the dancing
And a stillness as of sacring while the music plays
In unheard sweet, in unknown ways.
Ah, then, the march of destiny, that broke them, itself breaking,
Will usher in a movement cool as of the April wheat,
And the silence of the crowd will be as spirit's dedication
And its whiteness and its tension fitting prelude to the beat
The hushed stress of dancer's feet.
Then, to a music like forgiveness of all evil
The dancers of the proffered chance will glide into the light
The immortal thought of spirits will be ours for a moment
And the winter of our sorrow be an April of delight
If we will and do aright
With our memory brief as leaves and little hope and feeble sight.

169